BOLIVIAN DIARY
Ernesto 'Che' Guevara

Introduction by Fidel Castro

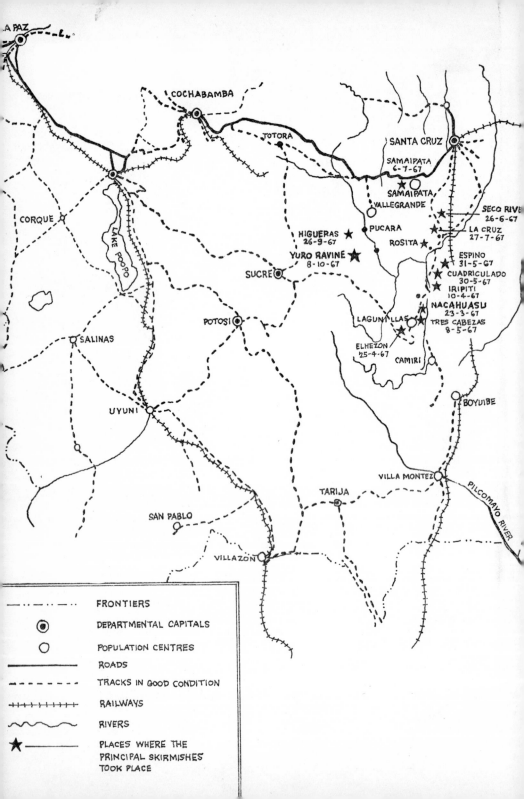

LA PAZ

COCHABAMBA

TOTORA

SANTA CRUZ

SAMAIPATA
6-7-67

SAMAIPATA ★
VALLEGRANDE

SECO RIVER
26-6-67 ★
LA CRUZ
27-7-67 ★

HIGUERAS ★
26-9-67

PUCARA

ROSITA ★

CORQUE

LAKE POOPO

ESPINO
31-5-67 ★
CUADRICULADO
30-5-67 ★
IRIPITI
10-4-67 ★
NACAHUASU ★
23-3-67

YURO RAVINE ★
8-10-67

SUCRE

SALINAS

POTOSI

LAGUNILLAS ★
TRES CABEZAS
8-5-67 ★

ELHEZON
25-4-67 ★

CAMIRI

BOYUIBE

UYUNI

VILLA MONTEZ

PILCOMAYO RIVER

TARIJA

SAN PABLO

VILLAZON

FRONTIERS

⊙ DEPARTMENTAL CAPITALS

◯ POPULATION CENTRES

ROADS

TRACKS IN GOOD CONDITION

++++++++++ RAILWAYS

〜〜〜 RIVERS

★ PLACES WHERE THE
PRINCIPAL SKIRMISHES
TOOK PLACE

BOLIVIAN DIARY

Ernesto 'Che' Guevara

Introduction by Fidel Castro

Translated by Carlos P. Hansen and Andrew Sinclair

Jonathan Cape/Lorrimer, London

First printing 1968

SBN 224 61620 X

Manufactured in Great Britain by Villiers Publications Ltd
London NW5

THIRD WORLD SERIES
edited by Marianne Alexandre

NOTE: This book is a translation of the official Cuban version
of the *Bolivian Diary,* published in Havana on June 26th, 1968,
in a free edition of 250,000 copies.

CONTENTS

A NECESSARY INTRODUCTION

It was one of Che's habits during his guerrilla life to jot down meticulously the day's events in a personal diary. On long marches, across rough and difficult terrain or through damp forests, when the lines of men, always weighed down with rucksacks and weapons and ammunition, stopped to rest for a moment, or when the column received orders to halt and pitch camp at the end of an exhausting day, Che (as he was affectionately called by the Cubans from the start) would be seen taking out his notebook and setting down impressions in his tiny, almost illegible doctor's handwriting. He later made use of the notes he managed to preserve, to write his magnificent historical reminiscences of the Cuban Revolutionary War, so full of value from a revolutionary, educational and human point of view.

Once again, thanks to Che's enduring habit of noting the principal events of each day, we have access to priceless information, detailed and rigorously exact, about those last heroic months of his life in Bolivia.

He constantly used these notes, which were not really intended for publication, as a tool with which to evaluate events, men and the general situation. They also provided an outlet for his acutely observant and analytical spirit, which was often tinged with a keen sense of humour. He kept up the habit so conscientiously that the notes remain coherent from beginning to end.

It must be remembered that this diary was written during extremely rare moments of rest from superhuman and back-breaking physical effort, without mentioning Che's exhausting responsibilities as a guerrilla leader during the difficult early days of this form of struggle, which unfolded in particularly hard material circumstances; this goes to show once again the kind of man Che was, and his strength of will.

There are detailed analyses of each day's incidents in this diary, exposing the errors, criticisms and recriminations, which are an inevitable part of any revolutionary guerrilla.

Criticisms of this sort have to be made incessantly in a guerrilla detachment, especially during the first stage, when there is only a small nucleus of men who are permanently exposed to extremely adverse material conditions and an enemy which is far superior in number; at such times, the least oversight, the most insignificant error of judge-

7

ment, can be fatal, and the chief has to be very exacting. He must turn each event or minor incident, however trivial, into a lesson for fighters and future leaders of new guerrilla detachments.

The training of a guerrilla force makes constant demands on the honour and conscience of each man. Che knew how to touch the most sensitive cords in a revolutionary's heart. When he told Marcos, after repeated warnings, that he might have to give him a dishonourable discharge, Marcos replied, ' I'd rather you shot me! ' Later on, Marcos bravely gave up his life. All the men in whom Che placed his trust and yet had to admonish for one reason or another in the course of the struggle, felt the same way as Marcos. Che was a humane and comradely leader who also knew when to be demanding, even severe at times. But he was always far harder on himself than on others and he based his discipline on the moral conscience of the guerrillas and on the tremendous force of his personal example.

There are numerous references to Régis Debray in the diary which show Che's great concern over the arrest and imprisonment of the revolutionary writer to whom he had entrusted a mission in Europe, although he would in fact have preferred Debray to stay with the guerrillas. This explains why there is a certain inconsistency about his attitude and why he even voices some doubts concerning Debray's behaviour.

Che never knew what Debray had to endure while in the clutches of the forces of repression, and the firm, courageous stance with which he confronted his captors and tormentors.

However, Che did realize the immense political significance of Debray's trial and, on October 3rd, just a few days before his death, during tense and bitter moments Che noted : ' We heard an interview with Debray, very bravely confronting a student who provoked him.' This was his last reference to the writer.

Just because Che often refers to the Cuban Revolution and its connection with the guerrilla movement, there are some who might interpret the publication of his diary as an act of provocation on our part, something that will give the enemies of the Revolution, the Yankee imperialists and their allies, the oligarchies of Latin America, a pretext for redoubling their attempts to isolate, blockade and attack Cuba.

Those who think this must not forget that Yankee imperialism has never felt the need for any excuse to carry out its misdeeds anywhere in the world, and that its efforts to destroy the Cuban Revolution date from the first revolutionary law promulgated in our country; for everyone knows that imperialism acts as a policeman for all that is reactionary and is the systematic promoter of counter-revolution, protecting the most backward and inhuman social structures in the world.

Yankee aggression may use our solidarity with the revolutionary movement as a pretext to attack us, but this will never be the true cause. To deny solidarity in order to eliminate the pretext would be an absurd, ostrich-like policy totally alien to the international nature of today's social revolutions. To disown our solidarity with the revolutionary movement would not just mean denying the pretext, but would actually be tantamount to supporting Yankee imperialism and its policy of world enslavement and domination.

Cuba is a small and economically underdeveloped country, like all countries which have been dominated and exploited by colonialism and imperialism for centuries. It is only 90 miles away from the coast of the United States, and has a Yankee naval base on its territory. There are many economic and social obstacles to its development. Our country has known periods of great danger since our victorious Revolution, but that will not make us yield or weaken; a consistent line of revolutionary conduct is impervious to hardships.

From a revolutionary point of view, we have no option but to publish the diary Che wrote in Bolivia. The diary fell into Barrientos's hands and he immediately sent off copies to the CIA, the Pentagon and the United States government. Journalists on good terms with the CIA were allowed to see the document in Bolivia and to have photostat copies made of it — but only after promising not to publish it for the time being.

The Barrientos government and its top military chiefs have good reasons for not wanting the diary to be published, since it shows up the incredible inefficiency of the Bolivian army, defeated over and over again by a handful of determined guerrillas who captured nearly 200 arms in battle within a few weeks.

Che also describes Barrientos and his régime in terms which they richly deserve and that cannot be erased from history.

Imperialism also has personal reasons of its own: Che and his extraordinary example are constantly growing in strength throughout the world. His ideas, his portrait and his name are banners in the struggle against injustice by the oppressed and the exploited and they arouse passionate enthusiasm in students and intellectuals everywhere.

Even in the United States, the Negro movement and the ever-increasing number of radical students have adopted Che's image. His photographs are paraded as emblems of the struggle in the most

9

militant civil rights marches and demonstrations against the aggression in Vietnam. Rarely, if ever, in history has one man's image, name and example spread so rapidly and so completely. The reason is that Che stood for the spirit of internationalism in its purest and most disinterested form, and it is this spirit which characterizes the world of today and, even more so, the world of tomorrow.

This amazing figure who symbolizes world-wide revolutionary struggle even in the capitals of the imperialist and colonial world came from a continent which was once oppressed by colonial powers and which is now exploited and kept in the most criminal state of under-development by Yankee imperialism.

The Yankee imperialists are frightened of Che's potent example and of everything that helps to spread his reputation. This is the greatest value of the diary: it is the living expression of an extra-ordinary personality, a lesson for guerrilla fighters written in the heat and suspense of each day. That is what makes it explosive; it is the proof that men in Latin America are not helpless against those who try to enslave them with mercenary armies; that is what has stopped the imperialists from publishing the diary.

It could well be that many so-called revolutionaries, opportunists and impostors of every sort, who call themselves Marxists, Communists and a variety of other names, would also prefer the diary to remain unknown. They do not hesitate to dismiss Che as a deluded adventurer, or at best an idealist, claiming that his death was the swan-song of revolutionary armed struggle in Latin America. ' If Che, the greatest exponent of such ideas and an experienced guerrilla fighter was killed in a guerrilla war and if his movement did not liberate Bolivia, that proves he was completely wrong! ' That is the way they argue; and how many of those miserable characters rejoiced at the news of Che's death, not even ashamed that their position and their reasoning coincided perfectly with those of the most reactionary oligarchies and with imperialism!

They reasoned like this to justify themselves or to justify treacherous leaders who did not hesitate occasionally to pretend to endorse armed struggle while in fact — as has been discovered since — their true purpose was to destroy guerrilla movements in the bud, to slow down all revolutionary action, and to put in its place their own absurd and despicable political deals, being utterly incapable of taking any other line of conduct. They also needed to justify those who lacked the will to fight and who will never fight for the liberation of their people, but who have turned revolutionary ideology into a caricature of itself, until it is nothing more than a dogma and an opiate without any genuine meaning or message for the masses. Such men have converted the organizations for the struggle of the masses into instruments of conciliation with both foreign and domestic exploiters and advocates of policies that go against the interests of the exploited Latin-American people.

Che envisaged death as a natural and probable part of the process, and he tried, especially in his last documents, to underline the fact that this eventuality could not slow down the inevitable march of Revolution in Latin America. He emphasized this in his message to the Tricontinental Congress: 'Our every action is a battle cry against imperialism . . . wherever death may surprise us, let it be welcome so long as our battle cry may have reached some receptive ear and another hand may reach out to pick up our weapons.'

Che looked upon himself as a soldier of the revolution and never worried about surviving it. Those who imagine that Che's ideas failed because of the outcome of the struggle in Bolivia might as well use this simplistic argument to say that many of the great revolutionary precursors and revolutionary thinkers, including the founders of Marxism, were also failures because they were unable to see the culmination of their life's work and died before their noble efforts were crowned with success.

In Cuba, the ultimate triumph of a process which was set into motion 100 years ago was not halted by the deaths of Martí and Maceo in combat, followed by the Yankee intervention at the end of the War of Independence which frustrated the immediate objective of their struggle, nor was it halted by the assassination of a brilliant theoretician of socialist revolution like Julio Antonio Mella, murdered by agents in the service of imperialism. And absolutely no one can doubt the rightness of these great men's cause and line of conduct, or the validity of their basic ideas which have always served as an inspiration to Cuban revolutionaries.

We can see from Che's diary how genuine was the possibility of success and what an extraordinary catalyst the guerrilla proved to be. On one occasion, observing obvious symptoms of weakness and rapid decline in the Bolivian régime, he noted: 'The government is disintegrating rapidly; what a pity we do not have 100 more men right now.'

Che knew from his Cuban experience how many times our small guerrilla detachment was on the point of being exterminated. It could have happened because, in war, one depends so much on chance and circumstances. And if it had happened, would it have given any-body the right to say that our line of conduct had been wrong, using our example to discourage revolution and inculcate people with a sense of helplessness? The revolutionary process has known setbacks many times in history. Did we not, in Cuba, experience Moncada only six years before the final triumph of our people's armed struggle?

Between the attack of July 26th, 1953, on the Moncada Fortress and the *Granma* landing on December 2nd, 1956, there were many who believed that the revolutionary struggle in Cuba was hopeless, that a handful of fighters would not stand a chance against a modern and well-equipped army, and that those fighters could only be looked upon as idealists and dreamers ' who were utterly wrong.' The terrible defeat and the total dispersal of the inexperienced guerrilla detach-ment on December 5th, 1956, seemed to prove the pessimists' point of view completely. . . . But, only twenty-five months later, the remnants of that guerrilla force had acquired enough strength and experience to rout the army totally.

There will be good excuses not to fight at all times and in every circumstance, and that will be the surest way never to win freedom. Che did not outlive his ideas, but he gave them added strength by shedding his blood for them. His pseudo-revolutionary critics, with their political cowardice and their permanent lack of action, will quite certainly live to see the day when their stupidity will be exposed.

It will be noticed in this diary that one of these revolutionary specimens becoming more and more common in Latin America, Mario Monje, brandishing his title of Secretary of the Communist Party of Bolivia, disputed with Che the political and military leader-ship of the movement. He went on to say that, for this, he would resign his party position, and seemed to think that it was quite enough to have once held such a title to claim the prerogative.

Needless to say, Mario Monje had no guerrilla experience and had never fought a combat in his life; without mentioning the fact that his personal notion of Communism should have rid him of such narrow and vulgar chauvinism long before then, just as our ancestors got rid of it to fight the first round for Independence.

If this is their concept of what the anti-imperialist struggle on this continent should be, then these so-called ' Communist leaders ' have not progressed further in the notion of internationalism than the Indian tribes which were conquered by the colonisers.

And so, this Communist Party boss proceeded to make ridiculous, shameful and undeserved claims for leadership in a country called

Bolivia, with a historic capital called Sucre, both named in honour of the first liberators who came from Venezuela; and Bolivia owed its final liberation to the political, military and organizational talent of an authentic revolutionary genius who did not limit his beliefs to the narrow, artificial and even unjust frontiers of that country.

Bolivia does not have an outlet to the sea; if it were liberated, it would need the revolutionary victory of its neighbours more than any other country so as not to be subjected to the most intolerable blockade. And Che was the man who could have accelerated the process with his tremendous prestige, abilities and experience.

Che had established relations with Bolivian Communist leaders and militants before the split that occurred within the Party, calling on them to help the revolutionary movement in South America. Some of those militants, with the party's permission, collaborated with him on various tasks for years. The party split created a new situation in which the militants who had worked with Che found themselves in different camps. But Che did not look upon the struggle in Bolivia as an isolated cause; he saw it as part of a revolutionary movement for liberation which would soon extend to other countries of South America. His aim was to organize a movement that would be free of sectarianism and that could be joined by all those who wanted to fight for the liberation of Bolivia and other Latin American countries subjected to imperialism. During the initial phase of preparation for a guerrilla base, however, Che had relied chiefly on the aid of a courageous and discreet group which remained in Monje's party after the split. It was out of deference to them that he first invited Monje to visit the camp, although he felt no sympathy for him whatsoever. Later, Che also invited Moisés Guevara, the political leader of the miners who had left Monje's party to help create another organization, from which he finally had to withdraw as well because he disagreed with Oscar Zamora. Zamora, another Monje, had agreed to work with Che in organizing armed guerrilla warfare in Bolivia, but he later withdrew his support and sat back like a coward when the hour for action had struck. In the name of 'Marxist-Leninism,' Zamora became one of Che's most vicious critics after his death, while Moisés Guevara unhesitatingly joined Che, as he had agreed to do long before Che came to Bolivia, offering his support and heroically giving up his life to the revolutionary cause.

The group of Bolivian guerrilla fighters, who had remained loyal to Monje's organization until then, did the same. Directed by Inti and Coco Peredo, who later proved their courage and their worth as

13

combatants, they broke away from Monje and became staunch supporters of Che. But Monje was not pleased with the outcome and began to sabotage the movement, dissuading militant and well-trained Communists from going to join the guerrilla. Actions of this nature show how incompetent leaders who are impostors and manipulators can criminally check the development within the revolutionary framework of men who are completely ready and able to fight.

Che was a man who never took any personal interest in rank, position or honours, but he was absolutely convinced of one thing: that in revolutionary guerrilla warfare, which is the basic form of action needed to liberate the peoples of Latin America given the economic, political and social condition of almost all those countries, the military and political leadership of the guerrilla has to be unified and the struggle can only be led from within the guerrilla and not from comfortable bureaucratic offices in the cities. He was determined not to give in on this point or to hand over to an inexperienced blockhead with narrow, chauvinistic views, the leadership of a guerrilla nucleus, which was ultimately destined to spread the struggle across all of South America. Che felt that chauvinism, which so often contaminates even the revolutionary elements in various Latin American countries, was something to be fought against, an absurdly reactionary and sterile attitude. As he said in his message to the Tricontinental: ' And let us develop a true proletarian internationalism . . . the flag under which we fight would be the sacred cause of redeeming humanity. To die under the flag of Vietnam, of Venezuela, of Guatemala, of Laos, of Guinea, of Colombia, of Bolivia, of Brazil — to name only a few scenes of today's armed struggle — would be equally glorious and desirable for an American, an Asian, an African, even a European. Each drop of blood spilt by a man in any country under whose flag he was not born is an experience passed on to those who survive, to be added later to the liberation struggle of his country. And each nation liberated is a phase won in the battle for the liberation of one's own country.'

Che also believed that fighters from different Latin American countries should participate in the development of the guerrilla and that Bolivia's guerrilla force ought to act as a school for revolutionaries who would learn in combat. To help him in this task he needed, along with the Bolivians, a small nucleus of experienced guerrillas, nearly all of them his comrades in the Sierra Maestra at the time of Cuba's revolutionary war; he knew the aptitudes, courage and spirit of sacrifice of these men, and not one of them failed him

14

in his demands, abandoned him or surrendered.

Throughout the Bolivian campaign, Che displayed those exemplary qualities of endurance, ability and stoicism, for which he was so rightly famous. It can truly be said that, knowing the importance of the task he had set out to accomplish, he proceeded to go about it with the most faultless sense of responsibility at all times. On every occasion that the guerrilla acted carelessly, he quickly took the fact into account, corrected it, and set it down in his diary.

The most incredible succession of adverse factors combined against Che, such as the loss of contact with a group of his fighters containing several valuable men, some of them ill, others convalescing. The separation, which was only intended to last for a few days, was drawn out interminably for months, during which Che made every effort to find them over extremely difficult terrain. During this period, his asthma became a serious problem; normally, a simple medicine would have kept it under control easily, but without that medicine, it became a terrible enemy which attacked him mercilessly. This occurred because the stores of medicine wisely stocked by the guerrilla were discovered and seized by the enemy. The evolution of the struggle was gravely affected by this event as well as by the liquidation, at the end of August, of the group with which Che had lost contact. Yet Che managed to overcome his physical deterioration with a will of steel, and he never allowed it to affect his morale or to stand in the way of action.

Che repeatedly came into contact with the Bolivian peasants and he could not have been surprised by their extremely wary and distrustful nature, as he had had dealings with them on other occasions and knew their mentality well. He realized that it would be a long, difficult and patient job to win them over to his cause, but he never doubted for a moment that he would succeed in the end.

If we examine the sequence of events carefully, we will see that even in September, a few weeks before Che's death, when the number of men on whom he could rely had dwindled drastically, the guerrilla still maintained its capacity for development and some of the Bolivian cadres, such as the brothers Inti and Coco Peredo, were beginning to show terrific potential as leaders. But the Higueras ambush, the only successful army action against Che's detachment, proved to be an irreversible setback for the guerrilla. This action killed off the advance party and wounded several men as they were moving in broad daylight to another zone where the peasants were more developed politically. This objective is not mentioned in the diary, but survivors have testified

15

that it was their goal. Of course, it was dangerous to advance by day along a road they had been following for several days, inevitably coming into contact with local people, in an area which was new to them. And it must have seemed obvious that the army would try to stop them somewhere along the way. But Che, fully conscious of the risk he was running, decided to try his luck so as to help the doctor who was in very bad physical shape.

The day before the ambush, Che wrote: ' We reached Pujio but there were people there who had seen us the day before, which means that news of us has spread by word of mouth.' ' It is becoming dangerous to march with the mules, but I want the Doctor to travel as comfortably as possible as he is very weak.'

The following day, he wrote: ' At 13:00, the advance party left to try and reach Jagüey and to make a decision there about the mules and the Doctor.' In other words, Che was trying to find a solution concerning the sick man in order to abandon their route and take necessary precautions. But that same afternoon, before reaching Jagüey, the advance party fell into the fatal ambush from which the detachment never recovered.

A few days later, encircled in the Yuro ravine, Che fought his last combat.

What this handful of revolutionaries accomplished remains extremely impressive. Even their struggle against the hostile environment they had selected is an unforgettable saga of heroism. Never before in history had such a small number of men set out on such a gigantic undertaking. Their faith, their absolute conviction that the great revolutionary process could be triggered off in Latin America, their confidence and determination as they went to accomplish this objective, give us some idea of their stature.

Once Che said to the guerrilla fighters of Bolivia: ' This form of struggle gives us the opportunity to turn ourselves into revolutionaries, the highest state a man can reach; but it also allows us to graduate as men; those who cannot reach either of these two states must say so and give up the struggle.'

The men who fought with him until the end proved they deserved both of these titles. They symbolize the kind of revolutionaries and men which history needs right now for a really difficult and arduous mission: the revolutionary transformation of Latin America.

During the first fight for independence, the enemy our ancestors fought was a decadent colonial power. The enemy which today's revolutionaries have to reckon with is the most powerful bastion of the

16

imperialist camp, the most highly advanced, technically and industrially. It was this enemy which re-organized and re-equipped the army of Bolivia after the people had crushed the previous repressive military forces. It was this enemy which immediately sent weapons and military advisers to fight against the guerrilla, just as it always has given military and technical aid to every force of repression on this continent. And if that does not suffice, this enemy intervenes directly and sends in troops, as happened in Santo Domingo.

You need the kind of revolutionaries and men that Che described to fight against such an enemy. Without such revolutionaries and men, ready to do what they did, without their spiritual strength to tackle the vast obstacles in their way, without their permanent readiness to die at any moment, without their profound belief in the justness of their cause, without their utter faith in the invincible strength of the people, faced with the might of Yankee imperialism as it throws its military, technical and economic weight around in every corner of the world, the liberation of the peoples of this continent will never be accomplished.

The people themselves in North America are beginning to realize that the monstrous political superstructure which governs their country has for quite a time been totally different from the idyllic bourgeois republic which its founders established nearly two hundred years ago. Their distress grows as they watch the moral barbarism of an irrational, alienating, dehumanized and brutal system which is making an ever-increasing number of victims among the citizens of the U.S., through aggressive wars, political crimes and racial folly; they see human beings turned into mere cogs of a machine; they see the disgusting way in which economic, scientific and human resources are squandered on a vast, reactionary and repressive military apparatus when three-quarters of the world is underdeveloped and hungry.

But only the revolutionary transformation of Latin America would enable the people of the United States to settle their private score with imperialism, while at the same time the growing revolt within the U.S. itself against imperialist policy could become a decisive factor in the revolutionary struggle of Latin America.

And if this half of the American continent does not undergo a profound revolutionary transformation, the fantastic inequality which presently exists between the two halves of the continent will continue to increase. This imbalance began at the turn of the century, when the U.S. rapidly industrialized, and at the same rate, acquired imperial aspirations as it followed the dynamic course of its own social and

17

economic evolution. Meanwhile, the other Balkanized nations of the American continent remained weak and stagnant, submissively yielding to the yoke of feudal oligarchies and their reactionary armies. In another twenty years, this terrible inequality will have increased a hundredfold, not just economically, scientifically and technically, but above all politically.

If this goes on, we will become progressively poorer, weaker, more dependent on, and enslaved by imperialism. This sombre prospect looms over all the underdeveloped nations of Africa and Asia as well.

If the industrialized and educated nations of Europe, with their Common Market and their pooled scientific institutes, are worrying about getting left behind and are afraid of becoming the economic colonies of Yankee imperialism, what does the future have in store for the people of Latin America?

Perhaps some liberal or bourgeois reformist or pseudo-revolutionary impostor, incapable of action, has found a solution to this genuine and incontestable situation which decisively affects the destiny of our people; if so, let him speak up. Let him tell us what he proposes in place of a profound and urgent revolutionary transformation, one which would polarize all the moral, material and human resources needed in this part of the world to make up for the economic, scientific and technical backwardness of centuries, even greater when we compare it to the industrialized world which makes us and will go on making us its serfs, especially the United States. If he can produce the magic formula which will accomplish this in a different way, which will wipe out the oligarchies, the despots, the petty politicians, all the lackeys of the Yankee monopolies, their masters, and if his solution can be applied as rapidly as circumstances require, then let him raise his hand and challenge Che.

But no one has proposed an honest alternative or a consequent line of conduct which would give genuine hope to the 300 million human beings, most of them desperately poor, who make up the population of Latin America; not forgetting that those 300 million will have become 600 million within the next 25 years, all of whom have a right to a decent living, a culture and civilization. It would therefore be more decorous to fall silent before the gesture made by Che and by those who fell at his side, courageously defending his ideas. Because of what that handful of men did, their noble ideal, which was to redeem a continent, will remain the highest proof of what will-power, heroism and human greatness can do. It is their example, which will awaken the conscience of the Latin American people in the struggle

18

to come; Che's heroic call will reach the receptive ears of the poor and the exploited for whom he gave his life. And many hands will stretch out to pick up weapons and to conquer freedom once and for all.

Che wrote his last lines on October 7th. On the following day, at 13:00 hours, in a narrow ravine where they had decided to wait until nightfall to break out of the encirclement, a large enemy troop made contact with them. Although reduced in number, the group of men who now made up the detachment fought heroically until dusk, from individual positions on the floor of the ravine and on ledges higher up, against the mass of soldiers who had surrounded and attacked them. There were no survivors among those who were fighting close to Che. Near him were the doctor, whose very bad state of health he had noted earlier, and a Peruvian fighter also in extremely poor physical condition; it therefore seems most likely that Che was doing everything in his power to protect the retreat of these two comrades to a safer place, until he himself was wounded. The doctor was not killed during this fight, but several days later, quite near the Yuro ravine. The guerrillas had great difficulty locating each other visually, because the terrain was so irregular and rocky. At times, they could not see one another at all. Some of the men, including Inti Peredo, who were defending the other entrance of the ravine several hundred metres from Che, held off the attack until dark and were then able to slip away from the enemy, heading for the spot where they had pre-arranged to meet.

It has been established that Che, although wounded, continued to fight until the barrel of his M-2 was destroyed by a bullet, making it totally useless. The pistol he was carrying did not have a magazine. It was only due to these incredible circumstances that they were able to catch him alive. The wounds in his legs, although not fatal, made it impossible for him to walk unaided.

He was taken to the village of Higueras and remained alive for another 24 hours, more or less. He refused to say a single word to his captors and slapped a drunken officer who tried to taunt him.

Barrientos, Ovanda and other top military chiefs met in La Paz and decided, in cold blood, to assassinate Che. The way they proceeded to carry out this underhand agreement in the school of Higueras is now known. Major Miguel Ayoroa and Colonel Andrés Selnich, two Rangers trained by the Yankees, ordered a non-commissioned officer, Mario Terán, to murder Che. Terán went in, completely drunk, and Che, who had heard the shots which had just killed a

19

Bolivian and a Peruvian fighter, seeing the brute hesitate said to him firmly, ' Shoot. Don't be afraid.' Terán left the room and his superiors, Ayoroa and Selnich, had to repeat the order which he finally carried out, firing his machine-gun at Che from the waist down. The official tale that Che had died a few hours after the combat was already in circulation; this was why his executioners gave orders not to shoot him in the chest or the head, so as not to produce instantly fatal wounds. Che's agony was thus cruelly prolonged until a sergeant, who was also drunk, finally killed him with a pistol shot in the left side. The whole procedure was in brutal contrast with the respect Che never once failed to show for the life of the many Bolivian officers and soldiers he had taken prisoner.

Those last hours of his life, spent in the hands of his despicable enemies, must have been bitter for him; but no man was better prepared than Che to face an ordeal of this kind.

We cannot, for the time being, reveal how this diary fell into our hands; it is enough to say that we did not have to pay anyone anything for it. It contains all the entries written down by Che from November 7th, 1966, the day on which he arrived at the Nacahuasu, until October 7th, 1967, the night before the combat in the Yuro ravine. Only a few pages are missing which are not yet in our possession, but they are entries for dates when nothing important happened, and they in no way alter the diary's overall contents.

Although there is not the slightest doubt about the document's authentically, all photostat copies of it were rigorously examined, not just to establish that they were genuine, but also to see if there were any discrepancies, however minor. The dates were also checked against those in the diary of one surviving guerrilla fighter. The detailed testimony of all the remaining survivors, who were present at these events, provided us with further proof of the diary's accuracy. We are utterly convinced that all the photostats were authentic copies of pages from Che's diary.

Che's wife and comrade, Aleida March, greatly helped in the laborious and exhausting task of deciphering his minute and difficult handwriting.

The diary will be published almost simultaneously by the publisher François Maspero in France, Feltrinelli in Italy, Trikont Verlag in the German Federal Republic and Ramparts magazine in the U.S.A. There will be Spanish editions by Ruedo Ibérico in France and Revista Punto Final in Chile, as well as in other countries.

!Hasta la Victoria Siempre! FIDEL CASTRO

20

NOVEMBER, 1966

A new stage begins today. We arrived at the farm by night. The trip has been quite a good one. After coming through Cochabamba, conveniently disguised, Pachungo[1] and I made the contacts and we travelled in two jeeps for two days.

When we got near the farm, we stopped the jeeps and drove up in only one of them, to avoid the suspicion of a farmer nearby, who mutters that our business is producing cocaine. The curious fact is that the ineffable Tumaini[2] is believed to be the group's chemist. Going to the farm on the second trip, Bigotes,[3] who had just learned my identity, almost drove the jeep over a ravine, and had to abandon it at the very edge. We travelled for about 20 kilometres, arriving at the farm after midnight, where three of the labourers are members of the party.

Bigotes is ready to work with us, whatever the party does, but he is loyal to Monje[4] whom he respects and seems to like. According to him, Rodolfo and Coco feel the same way; what we have to try to do is to make the party decide to fight. I asked him to help us and not to inform the party, until Monje, who is in Bulgaria, comes back; he agreed to both things.

We spent the day in the thicket near the stream, only about 100 metres from the house. We were attacked by a kind of *yaguasa,* very irritating even though they don't bite. The sort of insects we have found, up to now, are : the *yaguasa,* the gall-midge, the *marigui,* the mosquito and the cattle-tick.

Bigotes put his jeep back on the road with Argañaraz's help and arranged to buy some goods from him, such as pigs and chickens. I thought of writing to tell how things were going, but I left it for next week, when we hope to meet the second group.

---

[1] Also called by his other nickname, Pacho.

[2] Also called by his other nickname, Tuma.

[3] Also called by his other nicknames, el Loro or Jorge.

[4] Also called Estanislao, el Negro, or Mario. He must not be confused with the guerrilla el Negro, in the Joaquín group, who appears later on.

A day without news. We explored the area with Tumaini, following the course of the Nacahuasu river (really a stream), but we didn't get to its source. It runs between steep banks, and apparently the region is little visited. With proper discipline we can stay there for a long time.

In the afternoon, a rain storm drove us from the jungle to the house. I removed six cattle-ticks from my body.

Pachungo and Pombo went out to explore with one of our Bolivian comrades, Serafín. They got a bit further than us and reached the fork in the stream, a little gulch, which seems good. On their return they stayed hanging round the house and were seen by Argañaraz's driver, who was bringing back the men with some goods they had bought from him. I was extremely annoyed and we decided to move to the jungle tomorrow, where we will set up a permanent camp. It is all right if they see Tumaini because they already know him and he will pass for another hired man on the farm. The situation is quickly deteriorating; we'll have to see if we are allowed to bring our own men at least. I will feel at ease with them.

Nothing new today; spent all day in the other direction from the house at the new camp, where we slept.

The insects are infernal and we are forced to protect ourselves in our hammocks with a mosquito net (which only I have).

Tumaini went to visit Argañaraz and bought some things from him : chickens, turkeys. It seems that he does not suspect anything very much as yet.

Day without any news. We made a brief excursion to clear the ground for the camp assigned to the six from the second group, when they arrive. The chosen site is about 100 metres from the beginning of the main clearing, on a mound and near to a ravine where caves could be made to keep food and other things. By this time, the first of the three two-man groups, into which the section is divided, must be arriving. By the end of this week they will begin to reach the farm. My hair is growing, but very sparsely, the grey hairs are turning blonde and beginning to disappear; my beard is growing. In a couple of months I'll be myself again.

Sunday. Some hunters passed near our hide-out : Argañaraz's peons.
They are mountain men, young and unmarried; ideal for recruiting,
and they have a concentrated hate for their boss. They told us that
there are houses eight leagues further down the river, and that there
are some gulches with water. No more news.

One week in the camp. Pachungo seems sad and unable to adapt,
but he must get hold of himself. We started to dig today to make a
tunnel in which to hide any compromising stuff; we will conceal it
with a wood trellis and we will try to keep out the damp as much as
possible. We have already dug a hole one and a half metres deep and
started on the tunnel.

We continued with the tunnel; Pombo and Pachungo in the morning,
Tumaini and I in the afternoon. When we left work at six, the tunnel
was two metres deep. We think we will finish it by tomorrow and we
will put all compromising items in it. During the night, the rain
forced me to leave my hammock, which was soaked as the nylon
cover is too small. There wasn't any other news.

The tunnel is finished and camouflaged; we have only to conceal the
path there; we will take everything to our hut and tomorrow we will
hide it all, closing the mouth of the tunnel with a trellis of mud and
wood. The plan of this tunnel, numbered 1, is in Document I. Everything else as usual; I think that from tomorrow we can reasonably
expect news from La Paz.

We have put in the tunnel all those things which could be compromising for the people in the house, as well as some tins of food,
and it is quite well concealed.

There wasn't any news from La Paz. The boys in the house spoke
to Argañaraz, from whom they bought some goods, and he continued
to insist that they were helping to produce cocaine.

NOVEMBER 18

No news from La Paz. Pachungo and Pombo went back to explore the stream, but they are not very sure that it is the right camp-site. We will explore it with Tumaini on Monday. Argañaraz came to fix the road in order to get stones out of the river; he was busy at this job for quite a while. Apparently, he does not suspect our presence here at all. Everything goes along monotonously; the mosquitos and the cattle-ticks are beginning to give us ulcers in the infected bites. It gets a bit chilly at dawn.

NOVEMBER 19

No news from La Paz. No news here; as it is Saturday, hunters are about, so we stayed in hiding.

NOVEMBER 20

Marcos and Rolando arrived at noon. We are six now. They gave us the details of their journey immediately. It took them so long because they were only notified a week ago. They are the ones who travelled fastest by the Sao Paolo route. The other four will not get here until next week.

I was very impressed with Rodolfo, who came with them. He seems more determined than Bigotes to break with everything. Papi[1] informed him and Coco that I was here, breaking my instructions; apparently it is a case of jealousy in authority. I wrote to Manila with some recommendations (Documents I and II) and to Papi answering his questions. Rodolfo came back at dawn.

NOVEMBER 21

First day of the larger group. It rained a lot and we got soaked moving to our new spot. We are now settled. The tent was a truck cover which gets wet, but protects us a bit. We have our hammocks with nylon covers. Some other weapons have arrived; Marcos has a Garand, Rolando will be given an M-1 from the depot. Jorge stayed with us, but in the house; he will be in charge of the works there to improve the farm. I asked Rodolfo to find me a trustworthy agronomist. We will try to make this last as long as possible.

NOVEMBER 22

Tuma, Jorge and I reconnoitred the river (Nacahuasu) to explore the bed of the stream. With yesterday's rain the river was unrecognizable

---

[1] Also called Ricardo or Chinchu.

24

and it was quite hard to get where we wanted. This is a narrow strip of water which is difficult of access. If we make adequate preparations, it can be used as a permanent camp. We came back at about nine in the evening. No news here.

NOVEMBER 23

We set up a look-out above the little house on the farm, so that we would be warned of any inspection or undesirable visit. Two go out exploring, the rest have about three hours on guard. Pombo and Marcos explored the ground around our camp up to the stream which is still flooded.

NOVEMBER 24

Pacho and Rolando went out to explore the stream; they will return tomorrow.

This evening, two of Argañaraz's peons arrived unexpectedly for 'a visit.' There wasn't anything strange, but both Antonio,[1] who was with the scouts, and Tuma, who officially belongs to the house, were missing. Pretext : hunting. It's Aliucha's birthday.

NOVEMBER 25

From the look-out we were informed that a jeep with two or three people had arrived. They turned out to be from a medical service against malaria; they took blood-samples and left. Pacho and Rolando arrived very late in the night. They found the stream marked on the map and explored it; they also followed the main course of the river and found some abandoned fields.

NOVEMBER 26

Being a Saturday, we stayed in our hide-out. I asked Jorge to ride along the river to see where it went; the horse wasn't there and he left on foot to ask for one from Don Remberto (20 to 25 kilometres). By night time, he wasn't back. No news from La Paz.

NOVEMBER 27

Jorge was still missing. I gave orders to stand-to all night, but at 9 : 00 the first jeep from La Paz arrived. With Coco there came to stay Joaquín[2] and Urbano and a Bolivian : Ernesto, a medical student. Coco went back and also brought Ricardo with Braulio and Miguel

---

1 Also called Olo.
2 Also called Vilo.

25

and another Bolivian, Inti, to stay. We are now twelve insurgents and Jorge acts as the boss; Coco and Rodolfo will be in charge of contacts. Ricardo brought some disturbing news : el Chino is in Bolivia and wants to see me and send 20 men. This is not convenient because it will make the fight international before we have settled things with Estanislao. We arranged to have him sent to Santa Cruz, where Coco would pick him up and bring him here. Coco left at dawn with Ricardo who was to take the other jeep to continue to La Paz. Coco will drop by at Remberto's to find out about Jorge. In preliminary talks with Inti, he has given his opinion that Estanislao will not join us in our fight, but he himself seems decided to start on his own.

NOVEMBER 28

By morning Jorge hadn't turned up and Coco wasn't back either. They arrived later. All that had happened was that they had stayed at Remberto's. A bit irresponsible.

In the afternoon I spoke to the Bolivian group to inform them of the Peruvian request to send 20 men and they all agreed they should be sent, but after we were in action.

NOVEMBER 29

We went out to investigate the state of the river and to explore the stream where we will set up our next camp. Tumaini, Urbano, Inti and I formed the group. The stream is very safe but very gloomy. We will try to investigate another one which is one hour from here. Tumaini fell and seems to have fractured a bone in his ankle. We got to the camp at night, after mapping the river. No news here; Coco went to Santa Cruz to wait for el Chino.

NOVEMBER 30

Marcos, Pacho, Miguel and Pombo went out with orders to explore a stream further down; they will be gone for two days. It rained quite a lot. In the house, no news.

ANALYSIS OF THE MONTH

Everything has gone fairly well: my arrival was uneventful; half the men also got here without trouble, though they were a bit late; Ricardo's main collaborators will fight, come what may. The outlook appears to be good in this faraway region, where everything seems to indicate that we will be able to stay for as long as we think necessary. The plans are: wait for the rest of the men, increase the number of

Bolivians up to 20 at least and start operating. We still have to find out Monje's reaction and how Moisés Guevara's people will behave.

DECEMBER, 1966

DECEMBER 1

The day went by without news. By night Marcos and his comrades arrived; they made a bigger detour than was specified, keeping to the small hills. At two in the morning I was informed of the arrival of Coco and another comrade; I'll see to it tomorrow.

DECEMBER 2

El Chino arrived early, very outgoing. We spent the day talking. The important points : he will go to Cuba and personally tell them of the situation; within two months, that is to say when we have gone into action, five Peruvians will be able to join us; for the time being, only two will come, a radio technician and a doctor who will stay some time with us. He asked for weapons, and I agreed to give him one BZ, some Mausers and grenades, and to buy an M-1 for them. I also decided to give them support by sending five Peruvians to establish a link for getting arms to a region near Puño, on the other side of Lake Titicaca. He told me about his troubles in Peru; he also spoke of a very bold plan to free Calixto, which I think is a bit of a fantasy. He believes that some of the guerrilla survivors are operating in the zone, but no one knows for sure, as no one was able to get to the zone.

We spent the rest of the time exchanging anecdotes. He left for La Paz with the same enthusiasm, taking with him some photographs of us. Coco has instructions to set up contacts with Sánchez (whom I'll see later) and to get in touch with the president's chief of information, who is Inti's brother-in-law and has offered to keep us informed. The network is still in its infancy.

DECEMBER 3

No news. Being a Saturday, there is no exploration. The three peons went to make purchases at Lagunillas.

DECEMBER 4

No news. Everybody is quiet because it is Sunday. I am giving the men a talk about our attitude to the war and to the Bolivians who will soon come here.

No news. We thought of going out, but it rained heavily all day.
There was a false alarm when Loro fired some shots without warning.

We went out to start work on the second cave at the first stream. The
group was composed of Apolinar,[1] Inti, Urbano, Miguel and me.
Miguel is replacing Tuma who hasn't recovered yet from his fall.
Apolinar says that he is joining the guerrillas, but he wants to settle
some private matters in La Paz; he's been given permission, but he will
have to wait a little. We arrived at the stream at about eleven; we
made a camouflaged track and explored the ground to find a suitable
place for the cave, but there are stones everywhere, and the stream
dries up on its course through a gorge of solid rock. We put off the
exploration until tomorrow. Inti and Urbano set out hoping to hunt
deer, because we are very short of food and our stores have got to last
out until Friday.

Miguel and Apolinar found a suitable site and started digging the
tunnel; the tools aren't good enough. Inti and Urbano came back
empty-handed, but by evening Urbano had killed a turkey with an
M-1; as we had already had something to eat, we left it for breakfast.
Today really completes the first month of our stay here, but for reasons
of convenience, I will give my analysis at the end of each calendar
month.

We went with Inti up to a patch of solid ground at the top of the
stream. Miguel and Urbano continued digging the tunnel. Apolinar
replaced Miguel in the afternoon. By evening, Marcos arrived with
Pombo and Pacho, the latter a long way behind and very tired.
Marcos asked me to remove him from the advance party if he didn't
improve. I marked the way to the cave which is on Plan II. I left
them to do the most important tasks during their stay. Miguel will
remain with them and we will return tomorrow.

We went slowly back in the morning, arriving round noon. Pacho has

---

[1] Also called Polo.

orders to stay behind when the group returns. We tried to make contact with Camp No. 2, but we could not. There wasn't any other news.

DECEMBER 10

Day without news, except that we had the first bread baked in the house. I talked with Jorge and Inti about some of the most urgent tasks to be done. There wasn't any news from La Paz.

DECEMBER 11

The day went by quietly, but by evening Coco turned up with Papi. He brought Alejandro and Arturo and a Bolivian, Carlos. The other jeep remained on the road as usual. Later they brought the Doctor, Moro[1], and Benigno and two Bolivians, both ' Cambas '[2] from Caranavi's farm. We spent the night commenting as usual on their journey and on Antonio's and Félix's[3] absence, for they ought to be here by now. We decided with Papi to make two more trips to bring Renán[4] and Tania. We will dispose of the houses and depots, and give $1,000 to help Sánchez. He will keep the van and we will keep one jeep and sell the other to Tania. We still have to make one trip for weapons, and I ordered everything to be loaded in one jeep to avoid a switchover which can be spotted more easily. El Chino left for Cuba, apparently very enthusiastic and meaning to join us here when he returns. Coco stayed with us to go and look for food in Camiri, and Papi went to La Paz.

There was one dangerous incident : a hunter from Vallegrande saw some of our footprints and tracks, apparently spotted somebody, and found a glove lost by Pombo. This changes our plans and we must be very cautious. The man from Vallegrande will go out with Antonio tomorrow to show him where he set his tapir traps. Inti told me of his reservations about Carlos, the medical student, who, shortly after arriving, stated his views about the role the Cubans were playing and had said before that he wouldn't fight unless the Party fought. Rodolfo told him off because, he said, it was all due to a misunderstanding.

DECEMBER 12

I spoke to the group, ' reading aloud from the instruction manual,' about the realities of war. I underlined the need for unity of command

---

1 Also called Morogoro, Muganga or the Doctor.
2 Native of the eastern zone of Bolivia.
3 Also called el Rubio.
4 Also called Iván.

and discipline and I warned the Bolivians of their responsibility in breaking their Party discipline to adopt another line. I distributed the ranks as follows : Joaquín, as second-in-command; Rolando and Inti, as commissars; Alejandro, as chief-of-operations; Pombo, chief-of-services; Inti, finances; Nato, supplies and weapons; for the moment, Moro is in charge of medical services.

Rolando and Braulio went out to warn the group to lie low, to wait for the man from Vallegrande to set his traps or make an excursion with Antonio. They returned by night; the trap is not far away. They got the man from Vallegrande drunk, and he went away by night, very happy with a bottle of *singani* inside him. Coco went back to Caranavi's where he bought the necessary provisions, but he was seen by some people from Lagunillas who were amazed by the quantity of his supplies.

Later Marcos arrived with Pombo. Marcos had cut his eyebrow while chopping a piece of wood and had to have two stitches.

DECEMBER 13

Joaquín, Carlos and the Doctor went to join Rolando and Braulio. Pombo is going with them and has orders to return today. I ordered the track to be closed and another one to be made starting from the same place towards the river; we made it so well that Pombo, Miguel and Pacho got lost on their way back.

We spoke with Apolinar who will go back to his home in Viacha for a few days; we gave him some money for his family and reminded him of the need for absolute discretion. Coco said goodbye in the evening, but at about three in the morning there was an alarm because we heard noises and whistling and the dog barked; it was Coco who had lost his way in the forest.

DECEMBER 14

Day without news. The man from Vallegrande passed by the house to inspect the trap, because he had set it yesterday, despite what he had said before. We pointed out the new jungle path to Antonio so that he may take the man from Vallegrande through it to avoid any suspicion.

DECEMBER 15

No news. We started preparations for eight of us to go out and install ourselves permanently in Camp No. 2.

In the morning, Pombo, Urbano, Tuma, Alejandro, Moro, Arturo, Inti and I left for the camp, heavily loaded. The journey took us three hours.

Rolando stayed with us, and Joaquín, Braulio, Carlos and the Doctor went back. Carlos has proved to be a good walker and a good worker. Moro and Tuma discovered a cave near the river with quite large fish in it and they caught seventeen, which will give us a good meal; Moro wounded his hand on a catfish. We looked for a place to make a second cave, since we have finished with the first one, and all other activities have been stopped until tomorrow. Moro and Inti tried to hunt for a tapir and went out to spend the night looking for one.

DECEMBER 17

Moro and Inti only caught a turkey. We, Tuma, Rolando and I, spent the day digging the second cave which will be ready by tomorrow. Arturo and Pombo looked for a site to install the radio set and mended the entrance path which was in rather bad condition. It rained heavily throughout the night until the morning.

DECEMBER 18

It rained heavily all day, but we continued digging the cave; it is almost two and a half metres deep now, which is what we need. We explored a hill where we plan to install the radio set. It seems quite satisfactory, but we will have to test it.

DECEMBER 19

It rained again and we didn't go out, but at about 11:00, Braulio and Nato arrived with news that the river, although deep, could be crossed. As we left, we met Marcos and his advance party who were coming to install themselves. He is to remain in command and he has been ordered to send three to five men, depending on the circumstances. We made our way there in a little more than three hours.

At midnight, Ricardo and Coco arrived, bringing Antonio and el Rubio (they couldn't get a ticket last Thursday) and Apolinar, who is coming to join us definitively. Iván also arrived to deal with certain matters.

I spent practically all night without sleeping a wink.

We discussed various points and we were getting everything straight when the group from Camp No. 2 arrived, led by Alejandro, with the news that in the road near the camp there was a shot deer with a cord round its leg. Joaquín had passed through there one hour before, but hadn't said anything. We supposed that the man from Vallegrande had taken it there and for some reason had left it, and then escaped. We decided to post sentries at our rear and we sent two men to intercept the hunter if he appeared. A short while later the news came that the deer had been dead for a long time and was infested by worms. And later Joaquín came back and confirmed that he had seen it. Coco and el Loro brought the man from Vallegrande to see the animal and he stated that he had wounded it several days ago. This closed the incident.

We decided to speed up contacts with the man in the information bureau whom Coco has neglected and to speak with Megía so that he can serve as a contact between Iván and the man in the information bureau. He will keep in touch with Megía, Sánchez, Tania and the man from the Party who has not yet been nominated. He could be someone from Villamontes, but it has not yet been decided. We received a telegram from Manila indicating that Monje is coming via the south.

They have invented a contact system, but I am not very pleased because it clearly shows distrust of Monje by his own comrades.

At one in the morning we will get information from La Paz if they have already gone to fetch Monje.

Iván has the chance of doing some business, but his forged passport does not let him; the next stage is to improve the document and he must write to Manila to speed it up with our friends.

Tania will come next to receive instructions; I will probably send her to Buenos Aires.

We have definitely decided that Ricardo, Iván and Coco will leave from Camiri by plane and the jeep will remain here. When they get back, they will telephone to Lagunillas to say that they are there; Jorge will go by night to see if there is any news and he will fetch them if there is anything positive. At one in the morning we were unable to pick up any news from La Paz. At dawn they left for Camiri.

El Loro has not left me the plans made by the scout so I am now left without knowing what sort of road there is from here to Yaqui. We went out in the morning and made our way without any incident. We will try to have everything here for the 24th, the day we have planned a party.

On our way we met Pacho, Miguel, Benigno and el Camba going to fetch the generator. At five in the afternoon, Pacho and el Camba came back without the generator, which they had left hidden in the forest, because it was so heavy. Tomorrow five men will go and get it. We finished the cave for the goods; tomorrow we will start the one for the radio.

DECEMBER 22

We started the cave for the radio; at the beginning it was in loose earth and extremely easy, but soon we hit some hard stone which prevented us from going on.

They brought the generator, which is very heavy, but we have not tried it yet because we have no petrol. El Loro announced that he was not sending any maps because he had verbal information and he would come tomorrow to give it.

DECEMBER 23

We went out with Pombo and Alejandro to explore the ridge on the left. We will have to open a way through it, but it gives the impression that we can walk over it easily. Joaquín arrived with two comrades, announcing that el Loro was not coming because a pig had escaped and he had gone to look for it.

There is no news about the expedition made by the man from Lagunillas.

By evening we got the pig back; it is quite big but we have nothing to drink. El Loro is incapable even of getting these things and seems pretty disorganized.

DECEMBER 24

Day devoted to Christmas Eve. Some people made two trips and were a bit late but in the end we all got together and had a good time. Some of us had a few too many drinks. El Loro explained that the journey of the man from Lagunillas had not been very successful and had achieved only the few, imprecise results contained in the note.

DECEMBER 25

Back to work; there were no trips to the first camp. We have decided to call it C 26 as proposed by the Bolivian doctor. Marcos, Benigno

33

and el Camba went out and made their way up the ridge on the right. They came back in the afternoon with the news that they had seen a plain, two hours' walk from here; they will get to it tomorrow. El Camba came back with a fever. Miguel and Pacho made decoy routes on the left bank of the river and an access path to the radio cave. Inti, Antonio, Tuma and I continued with the radio cave which is very difficult as it is all stone. The rear party made their camp and found a look-out overlooking both sides of the access river; it is a very good place.

DECEMBER 26

Inti and Carlos went out to explore the point called Yaqui on the map; the trip is estimated to last two days. Rolando, Alejandro and Pombo continued the laborious work on the cave. Pacho and I went out to explore the paths made by Miguel; it is not worthwhile continuing the one along the ridge. The access path to the cave is quite good and difficult to find. We killed two vipers today and also one yesterday. Apparently, there are quite a lot of them. Tuma, Arturo, el Rubio and Antonio went hunting, and Braulio and el Nato stayed on guard at the other camp. They came with the news that el Loro had overturned his jeep, and with a note announcing Monje's arrival. Marcos, Miguel, and Benigno went out and tried to improve the path along the ridge; they did not come back all night.

DECEMBER 27

We went out with Tuma to try and find Marcos; we walked for two and a half hours up to a gorge coming down on our left flank to the west. We followed the footprints there, down rather steep cliffs. I was hoping to reach the camp that way, but hours went by and I did not get there. After five in the afternoon we got to the Nacahuasu, about five kilometres below camp Number 1, and at about 19:00, we got to the camp. We learned that Marcos had spent the previous night there. I did not send anyone to warn the others, assuming that Marcos had told them where I probably was. We saw the jeep which was quite badly damaged; el Loro had gone to Camiri to fetch some spare parts. According to el Nato, he had fallen asleep while driving.

DECEMBER 28

When we were setting out from the camp, Urbano and Antonio came looking for me. Marcos had gone with Miguel to make a path along the ridge to the camp and had not arrived; Benigno and Pombo went

34

out looking for me on the same road we had taken. When I got to the camp, I found Marcos and Miguel, who had slept on a ridge, as they were unable to reach the camp. The former complained about the way I had been treated. Apparently, the complaint was against Joaquín, Alejandro and the Doctor. Inti and Carlos returned without having come across anybody; they only found one abandoned house, which presumably is not the point marked as Yaqui on the map.

DECEMBER 29

We went with Marcos, Miguel and Alejandro to the barren hill to take a better look at the situation. It seems to be the start of the Pampa del Tigre, which is a chain of bare hills of uniform height situated at about 1,500 metres. The ridge to the left must be rejected because it curves towards the Nacahuasu. We came down and arrived at the camp in an hour and twenty minutes. We sent eight men to fetch the supplies, but they could not bring them all. El Rubio and the Doctor replaced Braulio and Nato. The former made a new path before coming; this path starts with some stones by the river and leads into the forest on the other side over more stones, which means no footprints are left. There was no work done on the cave. El Loro left for Camiri.

DECEMBER 30

In spite of the rain, which flooded the river, four men were sent to dispose of things left in Camp Number 1; it is now cleaned out. There is no news from outside. Six men went to the cave in two trips and put away everything that was supposed to be hidden.

We could not finish the oven because the clay was too soft.

DECEMBER 31

At seven-thirty in the morning, the Doctor came with the news that Monje had arrived. I went with Inti, Tuma, Urbano and Arturo. The reception was friendly, but tense. The question hung between us : What have you come for? ' Pan Divino '[1], the new recruit, was with him, so was Tania, who came to receive instructions, and Ricardo, who is now staying.

The conversation with Monje started with generalities, but soon came to his fundamental points, summed up in three basic conditions :

---

[1] Also called Pedro.

35

1. He would resign from the leadership of the Party, but he would at least obtain the Party's neutrality and would take cadres from it. for the struggle.

2. The political and military leadership of the struggle would go to him while the revolution was confined to Bolivia.

3. He would handle relations with the other South American Parties, trying to get them to support the Liberation Movements (he used Douglas Bravo as an example).

I answered that the first point was up to him as secretary of the Party, even though I considered his attitude completely wrong. It was vacillating and accommodating and protected the reputation in history of those who must be condemned for their weak stance. Time would prove me right.

I had no objection to his third point, nor to him trying to carry it out, but it was bound to fail. To ask Codovila to support Douglas Bravo was like asking him to condone an insurrection within his own Party. Time would also be the judge.

I could not accept the second point on any grounds. The military commander would be myself and I would not accept any ambiguities about this. Here the discussion ended and we talked in a vicious circle. We decided that he would think it over and talk to the Bolivian comrades. We went to the new camp and he spoke with all of them and gave them the alternative of either staying or supporting the Party; they all chose to stay and this seemed to be a blow to him.

At noon we drank a toast to mark the historical importance of the day. I answered, using his own words and marking this moment as the new *Grito de Murillo* of the continental revolution, and I stressed the point that our lives did not mean a thing, faced with the fact of the revolution.

Fidel sent the enclosed messages.

ANALYSIS OF THE MONTH
We have completed the team of Cubans with great success; morale is good and there are only small problems. The Bolivians are good, although few in number. Monje's attitude can slow down our development on one side, but it may contribute on the other side by freeing me from any political compromise. The next steps, apart from waiting for more Bolivians, are to talk with Moisés Guevara and with the Argentinians, Mauricio[1] and Jozami (Massetti and the dissident Party).

---

[1] Also called Pelado, el Pelao or Carlos.

JANUARY, 1967

In the morning, without previously discussing it with me, Monje announced that he was leaving and that he would present his resignation to the Party leaders on the 8th of January. According to him, his mission was over. He left looking like a man heading for the gallows. My impression is that when he found out through Coco of my decision not to give up strategic control, he stuck on that point to force a break, as his arguments are inconsistent.

In the afternoon, I grouped everyone and explained Monje's attitude, announcing that we would unite with all those who wanted to make the revolution, and I forecast difficult moments and days of moral anguish for the Bolivians; we would try to solve their problems by means of collective discussion or through the commissars.

I arranged Tania's trip to Argentina to interview Mauricio and Jozami and to bring them over here. We worked out the duties to be carried out by Sánchez and we decided to leave Rodolfo, Loyola and Humberto in La Paz for the moment, also leaving in Camiri one of Loyola's sisters, and in Santa Cruz, Calvimonte. Mito will travel through the Sucre zone to find out where he can set himself up. Loyola will be in charge of finance and has been sent 80,000 pesos, out of which 20,000 are for a truck that Calvimonte must buy. Sanchez will contact Moisés Guevara to have an interview with him. Coco will go to Santa Cruz to interview a brother of Carlos and put him in charge of meeting the three men coming from Havana. I wrote to Fidel the message contained in Document CZO#2.

We spent the morning coding the letter. The others (Sánchez, Coco and Tania) left in the afternoon, once Fidel's speech was over. He spoke about us in terms that create an even stronger obligation, if that is possible.

In the camp we only worked on the cave; the rest went out to get the things left in the first camp. Marcos, Miguel and Benigno went out to explore the north; Inti and Carlos explored the Nacahuasu until they came across some people, presumably in Yaqui; Joaquín and the Doctor must explore the river Yaqui to its source or until they meet people. They all have five days at the most.

Some of the men came from the camp with the news that el Loro had not come back after leaving Monje.

We worked without success in making a roof for the cave; we must finish it by tomorrow. Only two men went to pick up the load and brought the news that everyone had left last night. The rest of the comrades devoted their time to roofing the kitchen; it is finished now.

In the morning, Marcos, Joaquín, Alejandro, Inti and I went to the barren ridge. There I took the following decision : Marcos, with el Camba and Pacho, would try to get to the Nacahuasu on the right, avoiding all contact; Miguel, with Braulio and Aniceto, would look for a way over the ridge to try and make a central track; Joaquín, with Benigno and Inti, would look for a way to the Frías river, which according to the map runs parallel to the Nacahuasu, on the other side of the ridge, which must be the Pampa del Tigre.

In the afternoon, el Loro arrived with two mules which he had bought for 2,000 pesos; a good buy; the animals are strong and docile. We sent someone to fetch Braulio and Pacho so that he can leave tomorrow; they were replaced by Carlos and the Doctor.

After the class, I gave a little speech about the qualities of the guerrilla and the absolute need for a stronger discipline; I explained that, above all, our mission is to form a model nucleus as strong as steel; and for that, I explained the importance of study which is essential for the future. I then brought together the heads of the groups : Joaquín, Marcos, Alejandro, Inti, Rolando, Pombo, the Doctor, el Nato and Ricardo. I explained why Joaquín had been selected as second-in-command, due to some mistakes by Marcos which were constantly being repeated. I also criticised Joaquín's attitude in his incident with Miguel on New Year's Day and I then explained some of the tasks that have to be accomplished to improve our organization. When I finished, Ricardo told me of an incident he had had with Iván in front of Tania; in it, they swore at each other and Ricardo ordered Iván to get out of the jeep. These unpleasant incidents between comrades do a lot of harm.

The explorers left. The supply party was made up only of Alejandro and el Nato, while the rest devoted themselves to camp duties. We

---

1 The pages of the Diary which have not yet come into Cuban hands are the 4th, 5th, 8th and 9th January; 8th and 9th February; 14th March; 4th and 5th April; 9th and 10th June; 4th and 5th July.

took the generator and all of Arturo's things, then we made an additional small roof for the cave and we mended the well, also making a little bridge over the stream.

JANUARY 10

We made the change in the permanent watch at the old camp; el Rubio and Apolinar replaced Carlos and the Doctor. The river is still flooded, but it is going down. El Loro went to Santa Cruz and has not come back.

The Doctor (Moro), Tuma and I climbed the Pampa del Tigre with Antonio, who has to stay in charge of the camp. There I explained to Antonio his duties for tomorrow in searching for the possible stream existing west of our camp. From there, we looked for a connection with the old road taken by Marcos, and we found this relatively easily. Six of our explorers arrived at dawn; Miguel with Braulio and Aniceto, and Joaquín with Benigno and Inti. Miguel and Braulio found an exit to the river cutting through the ridge and followed it to another one which seems to be the Nacahuasu. Joaquín went down the river, which must be the Frías, and followed it for a while; this seems to be the same one that the other group followed, which indicates that our maps are very bad, because they give the impression that the two rivers are separated by some land and flow into the Grande separately. Marcos has not come back yet.

We got a message from Havana, announcing that el Chino and the doctor will leave on the 12th, and the radio technician and Rhea will leave on the 14th. It does not say anything about our other two comrades.

JANUARY 11

Antonio went out to explore the adjacent stream together with Carlos and Arturo; he came back at night, bringing only the news that the stream flowed into the Nacuhuasu by the hunting-ground. Alejandro and Pombo got to work drawing maps in Arturo's cave and came back with the news that my books were all wet; some of them were ruined and the walkie-talkie radios were wet and rusty. On top of this, two radio sets are broken; it gives one a most discouraging view of Arturo's aptitudes.

Marcos arrived at night; he had got to the Nacahuasu too far down and did not even reach its fork with what we assume to be the Frías. I am not at all sure of the maps or of the identity of this new waterway.

We have started learning *Quechua*[1], taught by Aniceto and Pedro. Day of the *boro*[2]. We took the flies' larvae out of Marcos, Carlos, Pombo, Antonio, Moro and Joaquín.

JANUARY 12

We sent the supply unit to bring in the last things. El Loro is not back yet. We did various exercises climbing the hills round our stream, but it took us more than two hours for the sides and only seven minutes for the centre; this is where we have to base our defence.

Joaquín told me that Marcos was hurt by my referring to his mistakes the other day at the meeting. I must speak to him.

JANUARY 13

I spoke to Marcos; his complaint was that he had been criticised in front of the Bolivians. His argument did not have any basis; except for his emotional state, which is worth caring about, the rest was insignificant.

He referred to expressions which Alejandro had used to run him down. This matter was cleared up with Alejandro, and it seems that it was only a bit of gossip. Marcos calmed down a little.

Inti and Moro went out hunting, but they did not catch anything. We sent groups to dig a cave in a place which the mules can reach, but this did not work, and we decided to build a little earth hut. Alejandro and Pombo made a study of the defence of the entrance and marked places for trenches; they will continue tomorrow.

El Rubio and Apolinar came back and Braulio and Pacho went to the old camp. No news from el Loro.

JANUARY 14

Marcos, with his advance party except for Benigno, went downstream to build the hut; he was not expected to return until nightfall, but the rain forced him back at midday without finishing the hut.

Joaquín directed a group that started digging the trenches. Moro, Inti, Urbano and I went to make a road round the limit of our camp along the ridge on the right of the stream, but we took the wrong way out and we had to cross some rather dangerous cliffs. It started raining at midday and activities were suspended. No news from el Loro.

---

1 *Quechua* is the native tongue of some Indians who live in Bolivia and Peru.
2 A fly which leaves its larvae in its bite.

I stayed in the camp, writing some instructions for the cadres in the city. Being a Sunday, we worked half a day; Marcos and the advance party on the hut, the rear party and the centre on the trenches. Ricardo, Urbano and Antonio went to improve yesterday's road, but they were unsuccessful because there is a cliff between the hill overlooking the river and the ridge.

The trip to the old camp was not made.

We continued with the work on the trenches, which are still unfinished. Marcos has almost finished building quite a good little hut. The Doctor and Carlos replaced Braulio and Pedro, who arrived with the news that el Loro had come back with the mules; but he did not turn up even though Aniceto went to fetch him.

Alejandro seems to have symptoms of malaria.

Day of little movement; we finished the front line trenches and the hut.

El Loro came to report on his journey; when I asked him why he had gone, he told me that he considered we took his trip for granted, and confessed that he had gone to visit a woman he has over there. He brought the harness for the mule, but he could not make it walk in the river.

No news from Coco; by now, it is a little alarming.

It was cloudy at dawn, so I did not make an inspection round the trenches. Urbano, Nato, the Doctor (Moro), Inti, Aniceto, and Braulio went on a journey for supplies. Alejandro did not work because he felt ill.

It soon began to rain heavily. El Loro arrived, soaked to the skin, to report that Argañaraz had talked with Antonio, hinting that he knew quite a lot and offering to collaborate with us on the cocaine or whatever it is, meaning by this " whatever it is " that he suspects that there is something else. I gave instructions to el Loro to commit him without offering much money; only cash for everything that he brings up with his jeep, and the menace of death if he betrays us. Due to heavy rain, el Loro left immediately to avoid being cut off by the river.

The supply unit had not come back by 8 :00, so I gave our men permission to eat their ration, which was devoured. A few minutes later, after some trouble in getting here, Braulio and el Nato arrived to report that the flooded river had cut them off on the way; they had tried to go on together, but Inti had fallen into the water, had lost his gun and was cut and bruised. The others had decided to stay the night there.

We started the day with the usual routine, working on the defences and improving the camp. Miguel fell ill with a high fever, which has all the characteristics of malaria. I felt blocked up all day, but the sickness did not break out.

By eight in the morning the four stragglers had arrived, bringing food supplies of corn on the cob; they had spent the night round a fire. We will wait until the river goes down to try and recover the gun.

At four in the afternoon, when el Rubio and Pedro had already gone out to replace the two men on guard in the other camp, the Doctor arrived, announcing that the police had been in the other camp. A Lieutenant Fernández and four policemen, in civilian clothes, had arrived in a hired jeep, looking for the cocaine factory; they only searched the house and noticed some irregular things, like the carbide brought for our lamps, which had not yet been taken to the cave. They took el Loro's pistol, but they left the Mauser and the .22; they ' pretended ' to take the .22 from Argañaraz, which they showed to el Loro, and they went off warning him that they knew everything and that he would have to reckon with them. Lieutenant Ferdández said that the pistol could be claimed back by el Loro in Camiri ' without too much fuss, talking directly to me.' He asked for the ' Brazilian.'

I gave instructions to el Loro to threaten the man from Vallegrande and Argañaraz, who must be the informers and spies, and to go to Camiri on the pretext of getting the pistol, in order to try and get in touch with Coco (I doubt that he is still free). They must live in the forest as much as possible.

I inspected the position and gave orders to carry out the defence plan explained last night. It is based on the rapid defence of a zone bordering the river, which depends on a counter-attack by some men in an advance party stationed parallel to the river which opens out on our rear.

We thought of doing some trial exercises, but the situation in the old camp is becoming more compromising, especially since a *gringo* with an M-2 appeared firing some shots; he is a ' friend ' of Argañaraz and has come to spend ten days' holiday at Argañaraz's house. We will send out groups to scout and we will move nearer to Argañaraz's house : if this blows up, before we leave the area we will make him feel our influence.

Miguel still has a high fever.

JANUARY 21

We fought a mock battle; it failed at certain points, but in general it was satisfactory. We must work harder on the retreat which was the weakest part of the exercise. Later the missions left; one with Braulio to the west to open up a route parallel to the river, another one with Rolando doing the same to the east. Pacho went to the bare hill to try out a walkie-talkie radio, and Marcos went off with Aniceto to find a road which will enable us to keep a close watch on Argañaraz. They all had to be back before two o'clock, except for Marcos. The tracks were made; so were the radio tests, which were positive. Marcos came back early because the rain interfered with visibility. Pedro arrived in the rain, bringing Coco and three new recruits : Benjamín, Eusebio and Walter. The first, who comes from Cuba and knows how to use guns, will go in the advance party, the other two in the rear. Mario Monje spoke with three men who were coming from Cuba and dissuaded them from joining the guerrillas. Not only has he failed to resign from the leadership of the Party, but he has also sent the enclosed Document IV to Fidel. I got a note from Tania announcing her departure and Iván's illness, and also a note from Iván which I enclose, Document V. I called the whole group together at night and read out the Document, pointing out the inaccuracy of points (a) and (b) of the plan of action, and I also took a firm line with them. Their reaction seemed good. Out of the three new recruits, two seem to be very firm and conscientious, and the youngest one is an *Aymará*[1] peasant who looks very healthy.

JANUARY 22

A supply group of thirteen people has left, along with Braulio and Walter to relieve Pedro and el Rubio. They came back in the after-

---

[1] *Aymará* : an Indian from the *altiplano* or table land.

43

noon leaving some things behind. Everything is quiet over there. On the way back, el Rubio had a dramatic but harmless fall.

I am writing a document to Fidel, the # 3, explaining the situation and testing our method of communication. I must send it with Moisés Guevara to La Paz, if he turns up at our meeting on the 25th at Camiri.

I am writing instructions for the urban cadres (Document III). There was no activity in the camp owing to the supply unit's departure. Miguel is getting better, but now Carlos has a high fever.

Today we made tuberculine tests. We shot two turkeys; an animal was caught in the trap, but it bit off one of its legs and got away.

JANUARY 23

We assigned camp duties and sent out some scouting groups : Inti, Rolando and Arturo went to look for a good hiding-place where the Doctor could eventually retire with a wounded man. Marcos, Urbano and I went to explore the hill in front of us, to find a place from where we can watch Argañaraz's house. We found it and there is a good view from there.

Carlos is still ill with the usual malarial fever.

JANUARY 24

The supply group left with seven men, coming back early with the entire load and some corn. This time, it was Joaquín's turn to plunge into the river, losing the Garand, which he later managed to recover. El Loro is back and already in hiding. Coco and Antonio are still out; they are due back tomorrow or the day after with Moisés Guevara.

We improved one of the paths which we will use to surround the enemy guards in the event of a defence from these positions. In the evening, we discussed yesterday's exercise, going over the various mistakes.

JANUARY 25

We left with Marcos to explore the path which would lead us to the enemy's rear. It took us over an hour to get there, but the location is excellent.

Aniceto and Benjamín went to test the transmitter from the hill overlooking Argañaraz's house, but they lost their way and were unable to establish communications; we will have to repeat the exercise. We started another cave for storing our personal belongings. El Loro arrived and joined the advance party. He spoke to Argañaraz,

44

telling him the things I had asked him to say. Argañaraz admits to having sent the hunter from Vallegrande to spy on us, but he denies having denounced us. Coco scared the hunter away from the house, since Argañaraz had sent him there to spy on us. We got a message from Manila, telling us that everything has arrived and that Kolle is going to the place where Simón Reyes is waiting for him. Fidel warns that he will hear what they have to say and that he will be severe with them.

JANUARY 26

Just as we had started work on the new cave, we heard that Moisés Guevara had arrived with Loyola. We went to the little house in our middle camp and they got there by noon.

I stated my conditions to Moisés Guevara : dissolution of the group, no ranks for anybody, no political organization yet, and no polemics about the subject of international or national disagreements. He accepted everything very sensibly and, after a cool start, relations with the Bolivians became friendly.

Loyola made a very favourable impression on me. She is very young and soft-spoken, but one can see a strong will in her. She is just about to be expelled from the Young Communists, but they are trying to make her resign. I gave instructions to the cadres, as well as a document; I also replaced what has been spent until now, which amounts to 70,000 pesos. We are getting short of money.

Dr. Pareja will be appointed head of the network and Rodolfo will come and join us in a fortnight.

I sent a letter to Iván (Document VI) with instructions.

I gave orders to Coco to sell the jeep, while still maintaining communications with the farm.

At nightfall, at about 19 : 00, we said good-bye. They will leave tomorrow night and Moisés Guevara will bring the first group between the 4th and the 14th of February. He said that he couldn't come earlier due to communications, and that many men were now going off for the carnival.

We will get some more powerful radio transmitters.

JANUARY 27

We sent a strong supply group which brought back almost everything. Coco and the messengers should leave at night; the messengers will stay at Camiri, and Coco will go to Santa Cruz to arrange the sale of the jeep, which is scheduled for after the 15th of this month.

We went on digging out the cave. We caught an armadillo in the traps. We are finishing the preparations for supplies on the journey. In principle, we will leave when Coco comes back.

JANUARY 28
The supply party cleared out the old camp. According to reports, the man from Vallegrande was spotted prowling around the cornfield, but he escaped. Everything indicates that we are reaching the moment when a decision will have to be made concerning the farm.

Supplies for the ten days' march are now ready and the date has been fixed : one or two days after Coco's return, on the 2nd of February.

JANUARY 29
A day of absolute laziness except for the cooks, the hunters and the sentry.

Coco arrived in the afternoon. He had not gone to Santa Cruz, but to Camiri. He left Loyola to go on to La Paz by aeroplane and Moisés to go on to Sucre by bus. Sunday was set as the day for making contacts.

The 1st of February was set for our departure.

JANUARY 30
The supply unit composed of twelve men brought most of the goods; but there is still a load for five men. The hunters did not catch anything.

We finished the cave for our personal belongings; it is not a very good one.

JANUARY 31
Last day of camp. The supply unit cleared the old camp and the two men on guard were relieved of their duties. Antonio, el Nato, Camba and Arturo stayed there with the following instructions : to make contact at least every three days; while there are four of them, two will be armed; the post must not be deserted for one moment; the new recruits will be instructed on general lines, but they must not know more than is absolutely necessary; the camp will be cleared of all personal things, and the weapons will be hidden in the forest, covered with a canvas; the reserve of money will stay in the camp all the time, to be kept on one of the men; the tracks already opened are to be patrolled as well as the streams nearby. In case of a rapid retreat,

46

Antonio and Arturo will go to Arturo's cave; el Nato and Camba will retreat through the stream, and one of them will run and leave a message in a place that we will select tomorrow. If there are more than four men, a group will guard the supply cave.

I spoke to the group, giving the final instructions for the march. I also sent Coco the final instructions (Document VII).

ANALYSIS OF THE MONTH
As I expected, Monje's attitude was evasive at first and treacherous later.

The Party is now taking up arms against us and I do not know what it will lead to, but it will not stop us and perhaps in the long run it will prove a good thing (I am almost sure of this). The most honest and combative men will be with us, even if they have to go through a more or less serious crisis of conscience.

Up to now, Moisés Guevara has responded well. We will see how he and his people behave in the future.

Tania has left, but there is no news of her nor of the Argentinians yet. Now begins the actual guerrilla phase and we will try out the group; time will tell what the prospects of the Bolivian revolution are.

The incorporation of Bolivian fighters has proved harder to accomplish than the rest of our programme.

FEBRUARY, 1967

FEBRUARY 1

The first stage is over. The men are a bit tired, but in general everything went all right. Antonio and el Nato came up to agree on the password, and brought my rucksack and Moro's, who is still convalescing from malaria.

We set up an alarm system in a bottle, which we left under a bush near the track.

In the rear party, Joaquín sagged under his load and slowed up the whole group.

FEBRUARY 2

Hard and slow day. The Doctor held up the march a little, even when our pace was already quite slow. At about four in the afternoon, we got to the last place with water and set up camp. The advance party was given the order to go as far as the river (presumably the Frías), but they were not keeping up a good pace either. It rained

47

during the night.

FEBRUARY 3
It was raining at dawn, so we delayed our departure until 8 : 00. As we were starting on the march, Aniceto arrived with the rope to help us cross the difficult passes, and a little later, it started to rain again. At about ten, we got to the stream, soaked through, and we decided not to go any further today. The stream cannot be the Frías river; it is simply not marked on the map.

Tomorrow, the advance party will leave with Pacho in front, and we will communicate every hour.

FEBRUARY 4
We walked from morning until four in the afternoon, stopping for two hours at midday to have some soup. The road followed the Nacahuasu; it is relatively good, but fatal for our shoes; some of the men are by now almost barefoot.

The group is tired, but has responded quite well up till now. I have been relieved of almost fifteen pounds and I can walk quite easily, even though the pain in my shoulders is unbearable at times.

We have not found any recent tracks nor signs of people by the river, but we are due to find inhabited areas any moment now according to our map.

FEBRUARY 5
Unexpectedly, after walking five hours in the morning (twelve to fourteen kilometres), we were told by the advance party that some animals had been found (it turned out to be a mare and its colt). We stopped and sent out scouts so as to avoid the place which was presumably populated. The discussion was whether we were at the Iripiti or at the fork with the Saladillo marked on the map. Pacho came back with the news that there was a large river many times bigger than the Nacahuasu, and that we could not cross it. We went up there and found the real Grande river, which was flooded besides. There are some signs of life, but rather old, and the roads we followed ended in the undergrowth where there were no signs of people passing by.

We camped in a bad place near the Nacahuasu, to use its water; tomorrow we will explore both sides of the river (east and west) to get to know the area, and another group will attempt to cross it.

48

Day of peace and of restoring our strength. Joaquín with Walter
and the Doctor left to explore the course of the Grande river; they
walked for eight kilometres without finding a ford, only a stream
with salty water. Marcos walked a little way against the current of
the river, but he did not get to the Frías; Aniceto and el Loro were
with him. Alejandro, Inti and Pacho tried to swim across the
river, but without success. We moved back nearly a kilometre,
looking for a better place. Pombo is rather ill.

Tomorrow we will start making the raft to attempt the crossing.

The raft was made under Marcos's direction; it was too big and not
easy to manoeuvre. At one-thirty we started to move towards the
river and at two-thirty we started to cross. The advance party
crossed in two trips, and in the third trip, half of the centre party
went across, taking all my stuff except for my rucksack. When
crossing again to get the rest of the centre party, el Rubio
miscalculated and the river swept the raft downstream, where it
could not be recovered. It was destroyed and Joaquín started
another one, which was ready by nine in the evening, but a night
crossing was unnecessary because it did not rain and the river
continued to ebb. From the centre party, the only people left to cross
were Tuma, Urbano, Inti, Alejandro and I. Tuma and I slept on
the ground.

Pretending to be Inti's assistant, I went to talk to the peasants. I do
not think we were very convincing due to Inti's shyness.

The peasant was a typical sort, capable of helping us, but also
incapable of realising the dangers that might crop up, and thus
potentially dangerous. He suggested various things about the peasants,
but he could not be precise because he felt rather insecure.

The Doctor treated the children; some had worms and another
one had been kicked by a mare; then we said good-bye.

We spent the afternoon and evening busily preparing *huminta*,[1]
(it does not taste good). At night, I talked to all of the comrades
together about the ten days to follow. In principle, I intend to walk
ten more days towards the Masicuri to make the comrades actually
see soldiers, then we will try to get back along the Frías to explore

---

[1] *Huminta*: a kind of bread made from corn flour.

another route.

(The peasant's name is Rojas.)

My father's birthday; 67   FEBRUARY 11

We followed a clearly-marked trail on the bank of the river, until
it was almost impassable and at times invisible, a sign that nobody
has been there for a long time. By midday, we got to a point where
we were boxed in completely near a big river, which made us wonder
if it was or was not the Masicuri. We stopped by a stream, and
while Marcos and Miguel went exploring upriver, Inti with Carlos
and Pedro went downriver, trying to locate its mouth. They did
so and confirmed that this is the Masicuri; its first ford seems to
be a little further down, where they saw some peasants loading their
horses. They have probably seen our footprints. From now on, we will
have to be extremely careful. We are one or two leagues from Arenales,
according to the peasant's information.
h = 760[1]

                                                             FEBRUARY 12

We rapidly covered the two kilometres travelled yesterday by the
advance party. From then onwards, the trail was broken very
slowly. At about four in the afternoon we got to a main road, which
seemed to be the one we were looking for. In front, on the other side
of the river, there was a house which we did not go to, and we
decided to look for another one this side of the river which must be
Montaño's, recommended by Rojas. Inti and el Loro went up
there without meeting anyone, even though the house's characteristics
indicated that that was the place.

   At seven-thirty we went on a night march which served to
demonstrate how much we still have to learn. At about ten, Inti
and el Loro went to the house again and did not bring back very
good news : the man was drunk and not very friendly : he only has
corn. He had got drunk in Caballero's house on the other side of
the river, where there is a ford. We decided to sleep in a nearby
thicket. I was terribly tired, because the *huminta* had disagreed
with me and I had not eaten anything all day.

                                                             FEBRUARY 13

At dawn it started to rain heavily and it lasted all morning,
flooding the river. The news was a bit better : Montaño is the owner's

---

[1] Reference to the altitude in metres.

son, about sixteen years old. His father was not there and would come back in a week. He gave us enough precise information about the ford a league or so from here. A portion of the road goes along the left bank, but it is short. On this bank there is only a brother of Pérez, a peasant whose daughter is engaged to a member of the army.

We went to a new camp by the stream near a cornfield—Marcos and Miguel made a path to the main road.

h=650 (stormy weather)

FEBRUARY 14

Quiet day spent in the same camp. The boy from the house came three times, once to warn us that some people had crossed the river from the other side looking for some pigs, but they did not come near us. We gave him some more money for the damage done to the cornfield.

The men with machetes spent the whole day slashing, without finding a house; they reckon they have prepared about six kilometres, half of tomorrow's job. We decoded a long message from Havana. Its main point was the news of the interview with Kolle. In the interview, he said that he had not been informed of the continental scope of the task; as this was the case, they would be willing to collaborate on a plan; they would like to discuss its details with me; Kolle himself, Simón Rodríguez and Ramírez would come. I am also informed that Simón has stated his decision to help us, regardless of what the Party decides.

They also informed us that the Frenchman, travelling with his own passport, will arrive at La Paz on the 23rd, where he will be put up at Pareja's or Rhea's home. There is still a part which we cannot decode for the moment. We will see how to face this new peace-making offensive. Other news : Merci turned up without the money, alleging a theft; we suspect he has misapplied funds, although it could be something even worse. Lechín will ask for money and training.

Hildita's birthday; 11   FEBRUARY 15

Day of easy marching. At about ten in the morning, we had reached the point where the trail-breakers stopped. Then everything went slowly. At five in the afternoon, a report came in of a cultivated field, and at six in the evening, it was confirmed. We sent Inti, el Loro and Aniceto to talk to the peasant, who turned out to be a certain

51

Miguel Pérez, the brother of a rich peasant, Nicolás, but he is poor
and exploited by his brother, so he is quite willing to collaborate with
us. As it was so late, we did not eat.

We walked a few metres to protect ourselves from the brother's
curiosity, and we camped on a hill overlooking the river 50 metres
below. The position is good for not being taken by surprise, but
it is a little uncomfortable. We started to prepare a large quantity of
food for the trip; we will cross the sierra towards the Rosita.
  In the afternoon, a strong and persistent rain, which continued
all through the night, delayed our plans, as it flooded the river and
left us once more isolated. We will lend 1,000 pesos to the peasant so
he can buy and fatten up pigs; he has a capitalist's ambitions.

It rained all morning. Eighteen hours of rain. Everything is wet
and the river is very flooded. I sent Marcos with Miguel and Braulio
to look for a track to get to the Rosita. He came back in the afternoon
after opening four kilometres of track. He reported that a barren
ridge rises similar to what we call the Pampa del Tigre. Inti is not
feeling well because of overeating.
h=720 (abnormal atmospheric conditions)

Josefina's birthday; 33
Partial failure. We walked slowly following the pace of the machete
men, but at 14:00 these had arrived at the open ridge where a
machete is not needed to cut a trail. We were delayed a little longer,
and at about 15:00 we arrived at a watering place where we camped,
hoping to cross the ridge in the morning. Marcos and Tuma went
out exploring and came back with very bad news; the whole of
the hill is cut by steep cliffs, impossible to descend. There is no other
course except to go back.
h=980

A wasted day. We went down the hill until we got to the stream.
We tried to go up along it, but it was impossible. I sent Miguel and
Aniceto to climb through the new counterscarp and to try to get
across, but they were unsuccessful. We spent the day waiting for
them and they came back announcing that the cliffs were exactly

of the same type, impassable. Tomorrow we will try to climb over the
last ridge beyond the stream which lies to the west (the others lie
towards the south and there the hill splits up).
h=760

Day of slow marching, full of accidents; Miguel and Braulio took
the old road to get to the spring near the cornfield; there they lost
their way and came back to the stream by evening. When we reached
the next stream, I sent Rolando and Pombo to explore it until they
got to the cliff. As they did not come back until three, we followed
the road that Marcos was making, leaving Pedro and el Rubio to
wait for them. We arrived at four-thirty at the spring near the
cornfield, where we set up camp. The explorers did not come back.
h=720

Slow walk upstream. Pombo and Rolando came back with the news
that the other stream could be crossed, but Marcos explored this
and it looked just the same as the others. We left at eleven in the
morning, but at one-thirty in the afternoon we came across some
pools full of icy water, which could not be forded. We sent el Loro to
explore, but it took him a long time, so I sent Braulio and Joaquín
from the rear party. El Loro came with the news that the stream
widened a bit further up and was perhaps easier to cross. This made
us decide to go on without waiting for Joaquín's report. At six in
the evening, we camped, when the latter brought the news that the
ridge could be climbed and there was quite a good way up. Inti is
not at all well; he has stomach trouble for the second time this week.
h=860

The whole day was spent climbing quite difficult ridges covered in
thick undergrowth. After an exhausting day, we camped without
getting to the top, so I sent Joaquín and Pedro to try to make it on
their own. They came back at seven with the news that it would
take at least three hours more to reach our goal. We are at the sources
of the stream which flows out into the Masicuri, but in a southerly
direction.
h=1,180

A black day for me. I made it, but I am completely exhausted. In
the morning Marcos, Braulio and Tuma set off to prepare the trail
while we waited at the camp. There we deciphered a new message,
which announced that my message had been received through the
French letter-box. At 12 :00, we left under a sun hot enough to crack
stones, and shortly afterwards, as we were getting to the top of the
highest hill, I almost fainted; from then onwards I walked on will-
power alone. The maximum height of the area is 1,420 metres; there
is an overlook above a vast area including the Grande river, the
mouth of the Nacahuasu and part of the Rosita. The topography
is different from that shown on the map. After a clear dividing line,
it goes down abruptly to a sort of tree-topped plateau about eight
or ten kilometres wide, ending in the course of the Rosita; then
another mountain chain rises to much the same height as this chain,
and in the distance, plains are visible.

We decided to come down through a practicable but quite steep
place, so we could follow a stream leading to the Grande river and
go from there to the Rosita. Apparently there are no houses on the
banks, contrary to what is shown on the map. We camped at 900
metres, after an infernal descent without water and in the dusk.

At dawn yesterday, I overheard Marcos telling a comrade to fuck
off and during the day he said it to another man. I must speak
with him.

Ernestico's birthday; 2
Painful and discouraging day. We advanced very little. There is no
water, because the creek we are following is dry. At 12 :00 the exhausted machete men were replaced; at two, it was raining a little and
we filled the canteens; a bit later we found a well, and at five in the
afternoon we camped in a clearing by the water. Marcos and
Urbano continued exploring and Marcos came back with the news
that the river was only a couple of kilometres away, but that the
road by the stream was a very bad one turning into a swamp.
h=680

A black day. We made very little progress, and, on top of that,
Marcos missed the route and we lost all morning; he had gone out
with Miguel and el Loro. At noon he reported this and asked to
be relieved and to have communications equipment; Braulio, Tuma

and Pacho went there. At two in the afternoon, Pacho came back saying that Marcos had sent him because they could not hear very well. At four-thirty in the afternoon, I sent Benigno to warn Marcos to come back by six in the evening, if he did not find the river. After Benigno had left, Pacho called to tell me that he and Marcos had had an argument and that Marcos had given him arbitrary orders, threatening him with a machete and using its handle to hit him in the face. When Pacho went back and told him not to go on, he threatened him again with the machete and shook him and tore his clothes.

Faced with this serious matter, I called Inti and Rolando. They confirmed the bad feeling existing in the advance party due to Marcos's temper, but they also reported some of Pacho's indiscretions.

FEBRUARY 26

In the morning I had a talk with Marcos and Pacho. This convinced me that Marcos was to blame for the insult and the maltreatment and perhaps even the threat with the machete, but certainly not for the blow. There were also some insulting answers from Pacho, since he has a tendency towards bravado, which he has shown before. I waited until everyone was grouped and I told them then of the importance of our attempt to get to the Rosita, explaining how this form of hardship was only an introduction to what we would suffer. I explained that, because we were not adapted to this life, disgraceful incidents could happen like the one between the two Cubans; I criticized Marcos for his attitude and I warned Pacho that one more incident of this sort would mean a dishonourable discharge from the guerrilla. Pacho, besides refusing to go on operating the radio set, had come back without telling me about the incident, and later he most probably lied to me about Marcos hitting him.

I told the Bolivians that anyone not feeling up to it should not be devious, but should just tell me and we would let him go freely.

We continued walking, trying to reach the Grande river. We made it and we were able to follow it for a little more than one kilometre, but we had to climb again because the river flowed past a cliff. Benjamín fell behind because of difficulties with his rucksack and physical exhaustion; when he came up to us, I gave him orders to carry on and he did so. He walked about 50 metres, but he lost the trail up. As he was looking for it along a ledge, and as I was ordering Urbano to tell him the way, he made a sudden movement and fell into the water. He did not know how to swim. The current

55

was very strong and swept him away while he was still touching bottom; we rushed to his help and, while we were taking our things off, he disappeared in a whirlpool. Rolando swam out there and tried to dive, but the current swept him far away. After five minutes, we gave up all hope for Benjamín. He was a weak boy and very unfit, although he had tremendous will-power; the test was stronger than him; his physical qualities did not match his will, and we have now had our baptism of death on the banks of the Grande river in a most absurd manner. We camped without getting to the Rosita, at about five in the afternoon. We ate our last ration of kidney beans.

FEBRUARY 27

After another tiring day, walking along the banks and climbing cliffs, we reached the Rosita river. It is bigger than the Nacahuasu, but smaller than the Masicuri, and its waters are reddish. We ate our last reserve ration and we did not find any nearby signs of life, even though we are quite near to main roads and populated areas. h=600

FEBRUARY 28

A half-day of rest. After breakfast (tea), I gave a short speech analysing Benjamín's death and narrating some anecdotes from the Sierra Maestra. After that the explorers left; Miguel, Inti and el Loro went up the Rosita, with instructions to walk for three and a half hours, the time I thought it would take to reach the Abaposito river. But they did not make it, for they could not find a track. They did not find any recent signs of life. Joaquín and Pedro climbed the hills facing us, but they did not find anything, neither a path nor any signs of one. Alejandro and el Rubio crossed the river and did not find a track, although their exploration was only superficial. Marcos supervised the construction of a raft and we began crossing as soon as this was finished. We crossed a bend of the river where the Rosita meets the Abaposito. We took across the rucksacks of five men including Miguel's, but Benigno's was lost—exactly the reverse of what happened to them, and on top of all this, Benigno left his shoes behind.

The raft could not be recovered, and as the second one was not finished, we put off the crossing until the morning.

ANALYSIS OF THE MONTH
Although I have now news of what has happened in the camp,

56

everything is going reasonably well, with some exceptions, which are
fatal in these cases.

From the outside, there is no news about the two men who were
to be sent to me to complete the group; the Frenchman must already
be in La Paz and will reach the camp any day now; I have no news
from the Argentinians or from el Chino; the messages get through
well in both directions; the Party's attitude continues to be two-faced
and hesitant, to say the least, although there is still one point to clear
up, which may be decisive, when I speak with the new delegation.

The march went quite well except for the accident that cost
Benjamín's life; the men are still weak and not all the Bolivians
will last out. The past days of hunger have shown a weakening
of enthusiasm, which becomes more evident when we are divided.

Of the Cubans, two of the ones without much experience, Pacho
and el Rubio, have not responded well yet, but Alejandro has done
very well; of the old ones, Marcos gives me continuous headaches
and Ricardo is not doing his best. The others are all right.

The next stage will be that of combat and certainly decisive.

MARCH, 1967

MARCH 1

It started to rain at six in the morning. We postponed the crossing,
waiting for the rain to stop, but it got worse and went on until three
in the afternoon; the river was rising and we decided that it would
be wiser not to attempt the crossing. It is now very flooded and shows
no signs of ebbing soon. I went to an abandoned hut to escape from
the water and we camped there. Joaquín stayed in the same place.
In the evening, he reported to me that Polo had taken his can of
milk and Eusebio his milk and sardines. For the time being, as a
punishment, they will not eat these foods when the others do. It is a
bad sign.

MARCH 2

At dawn, it was raining and the men were out of sorts, including
me. The river was even more flooded. We decided to leave the camp
as soon as the sky cleared and to continue parallel to the river by the
way we came. We left at noon and supplied ourselves with the
hearts of a tropical palm, *palmito de corojo*. At four-thirty we
stopped, because we had lost our way trying to cut through an old
track which came to an end. We have not yet had any news from
the advance party.

We started enthusiastically, keeping up a good pace, but the hours
slowed us down and we had to cut our way through the ridge
because I feared an accident in the area where Benjamín fell. It took
us four hours to cover the same ground that we had done in less
than half an hour down below. At 18 : 00 we got to the river bank
where we camped, but as we only had two palm hearts left, Miguel
and Urbano and then Braulio went to look for some more further
away, returning at 21 : 00. At about midnight we ate; the palm hearts
(known as *totai* in Bolivia) are saving the situation.
h = 600

Miguel and Urbano left in the morning and spent all day with their
machetes on the trail, coming back at about six in the evening; they
advanced about five kilometres and saw a plain which must make
our advance easier; but there is no place for a camp, so we
decided to stay here until we enlarged the track. The hunters got
two little monkeys, a parrot and a dove; this was our meal together
with the palm hearts, abundant by the stream.

The men's morale is low and their physical condition is
deteriorating every day. My legs are beginning to show signs of
oedema.

Joaquín and Braulio went out to break a trail. It was raining and
they were both so weak that they could not make much progress.
We collected twelve palm hearts and shot some small birds, which
allows us to keep the tins one more day and make up a reserve of
palm hearts for two days.

Day of intermittent marching until five in the afternoon. Miguel,
Urbano and Tuma are the machete men. We advance a little and
in the distance we see some ridges which seem to be the ones by the
Nacahuasu. We only shot a small parrot, which we gave to the rear
party. Today, we ate palm hearts with meat. We only have three
scant meals left.
h = 600

Four months up. The morale of the men is sinking as the supplies
come to an end, but not the trail. We advanced today some four
or five kilometres along the river bank and found a promising trail
at last. The meal : three and a half little birds and the rest of the
palm hearts. From tomorrow onwards, tins only, a third of a tin
per head for two days; then the tinned milk, which is the last thing
we have got. We must be at least two or three days from the
Nacahuasu.
h=610

Little progress today, with many surprises and much suspense. We
left the camp at ten in the morning without waiting for Rolando,
who was out hunting. We walked for only an hour and a half before
we reached the machete men and the hunters (Urbano, Miguel,
Tuma—the Doctor and Chinchu, respectively). They had a heap
of parrots, but they had halted because they had found a water
main. I gave orders to camp there, and I went to prospect what
turned out to be an oil pumping station. Inti and Ricardo plunged
into the water; they had to pretend to be hunters. They went in with
their clothes on, trying to get across in two stages; but Inti got into
trouble and nearly drowned himself. Ricardo helped him and they
finally reached the far bank after attracting everybody's attention.
They did not give the danger signal and just disappeared. They had
started to cross at noon, and at quarter past three I finally withdrew,
still without any news of them. The afternoon went by, and they did
not show up. The last sentry returned at nine in the evening, and they
still had given no signal.

I was very worried; two brave comrades were exposed to danger
and we did not know what had happened to them. We decided that
the two best swimmers, Alejandro and Rolando, should swim across
tomorrow at daybreak.

We ate better than on the previous days, although we had no palm
hearts, because of all the parrots and the two monkeys killed by
Rolando.

We started to prepare for an early crossing, but we had to build a
raft, which delayed us for some time. The sentry announced that he
had seen some half-naked people on the far bank; it was 8 :30

59

and our crossing was put off. A trail has been made which leads to
a clearing on the other side, but we could be seen, so that we will
have to leave very early next morning under cover of the river
mist. At about 16 : 00, after a long and maddening watch that had
lasted since 10 : 30 for me, the men after supplies (Inti and
Chinchu) plunged into the river and came out far below us. They
brought back a pig, bread, rice, sugar, coffee, some tins, some
fermented corn, *etc*. We gave ourselves a little feast of coffee and
bread, and I authorized the opening of a tin of condensed milk
from our reserve to make a sweet.[1] They explained that they had
been showing themselves every hour, but they had not been seen
by us. Marcos and his men had passed three days ago, and apparently
he was up to his tricks and showed the guns. The engineers of the
oil station are not sure of the distance to the Nacahuasu, but they
think it is about a five days' journey. The supplies will not last, if
this is so. The pump is part of a pumping plant which is being built.

MARCH 10

We left at about 6 : 30, and caught up with the machete men
three-quaters of an hour later. At 8 : 00, it began to rain and
continued until 11 : 00. In all, we walked for about three hours,
camping at about 17 : 00. We can spot some hills which might
be the Nacahuasu. Braulio went out to explore and came back with
the news that there is a trail and that the river runs straight to the
west.
h = 600

MARCH 11

The day began well. We walked for more than an hour along a
perfect track, but it suddenly came to an end. Braulio got his
machete and cut his way laboriously until he reached the bank of
the river. We waited a while for him and Urbano to open up the
way, and when we were about to go on, the flood cut off our path
in a matter of seconds, and the river rose almost a couple of metres.

We were isolated from the machete men and were forced to push
on through the forest. At one-thirty we halted, and I sent Miguel and
Tuma with instructions to contact the advance party and to transmit
orders for its return, if it had not managed to get to the Nacahuasu

---

1 Condensed milk, boiled or heated to become *Dulce de Leche,* is very popular
in Argentina.

60

or another good spot.

They came back at six in the afternoon; they had progressed some three kilometres before coming to a very steep cliff. Apparently we are near, but the last days are going to be very hard if the river does not go down, which seems highly improbable. We covered four to five kilometres.

A disagreeable incident took place because the rear party is short of sugar and the men suspect that they have been given short rations or else that Braulio has been helping himself. I must speak with him. h=610

MARCH 12

We covered the track cleared yesterday in one hour and ten minutes. When we arrived, Miguel and Tuma, who had gone ahead, were already looking for ways to bypass the steep cliff. We spent the whole day doing this; our only activity was to shoot four small birds which we ate to supplement the rice with mussels. We have two meals left. Miguel stayed on the other side and he seems to have found a way to the Nacahuasu. We travelled about three to four kilometres.

MARCH 13

From six-thirty till noon we went up and down some hellish cliffs, following the way made by Miguel in a herculean task. We thought we had almost reached the Nacahuasu when we ran across some bad passes, and in five hours we made little real progress. We camped under a heavy shower which let up at five o'clock. The men are rather tired and demoralized again. Only one meal left. We travelled about six kilometres without much point.

MARCH 15

Only we, the centre party, crossed the river, with the help of el Rubio and the Doctor. We wanted to get to the mouth of the Nacahuasu, but three of the men cannot swim and we are heavily laden. The current carried us along nearly a kilometre, and the raft could not be used as we had intended. Eleven of us stayed on this side and tomorrow the Doctor and el Rubio will cross again. We shot four hawks for our meal; they were not as bad as might be imagined. Everything has got soaked, and the weather continues to be very wet. The men's morale is low; Miguel has swollen feet and some of the others suffer from the same condition. h=580

We decided to eat the horse, as our swellings are alarming. Miguel, Inti, Urbano and Alejandro show various symptoms; I am extremely weak. We made a mistake in our calculations, since we believed that Joaquín would get through, but this was not so. The Doctor and el Rubio tried to get across the river to help him and they were swept downriver, out of our sight. Joaquín asked permission to cross and was given it; but his party was also swept downriver. I sent Pombo and Tuma to fetch them, but they could not find them and came back at night. From five o'clock on, we had an orgy of horsemeat. Tomorrow there will probably be consequences. According to my calculations, Rolando should be reaching the camp today.

We decoded the whole of message No. 32 which announced the arrival of a Bolivian, who will join us, bringing another load of glucantine and antiparasitic (leismania). Up till now, we haven't had any cases of this.

Once again a tragedy before the actual fighting starts. Joaquín appeared at mid-morning; Miguel and Tuma had gone to meet him with some good pieces of meat. Their odyssey had been serious : they could not control the raft and it was carried down the Nacahuasu, until they reached a whirlpool which overturned them several times by their account. The final result was the loss of several rucksacks, almost all the bullets, six guns and one man : Carlos. He and Braulio were sucked into the whirlpool, but their fate was not the same : Braulio reached the bank and could see Carlos being dragged along, unable even to struggle. Joaquín was up ahead with all his men and did not see him go by. Up till now, Carlos was considered the best of the Bolivians in the rear party, due to his seriousness, discipline and enthusiasm.

The lost weapons are : one Brno, belonging to Braulio; two M-1s, Carlos's and Pedro's; three Mausers, Abel's, Eusebio's and Polo's. Joaquín reported that he had seen the Doctor and el Rubio on the other bank and had ordered them to make a raft and come across. At 14 :00 they appeared, having had their share of trials and perils; they were naked and el Rubio barefoot. Their raft had been destroyed by the first whirlpool. They came ashore almost exactly where we had.

Our departure is set for early tomorrow morning, and Joaquín will leave by midday. I do hope to get some news during the day tomorrow. The morale of Joaquín's men seems good.

We set off early, leaving Joaquín to digest and finish preparing his
half of the horse, with instructions to move on as soon as he felt
strong enough. I had a fight to keep some of the meat in reserve,
because the opinion of the men was that it should all be eaten. By
mid-morning Ricardo, Inti, and Urbano were lagging behind, and
we had to wait for them, which went against my plan to rest in the
camp from which we had set off on the journey out. Anyway, we
made slow progress.

At 14 : 30 Urbano came in with a small deer shot by Ricardo;
this gives us some leeway and allows us to keep the horse ribs in
reserve. At 16:30 we reached the mid-point of our intended day's
march; but we slept there. Some of the men are grumbling and bad-
tempered : Chinchu, Urbano and Alejandro.

We at the front travelled well in the morning, halting at 11 :00 as we
had agreed, but Ricardo, Urbano, and this time Alejandro, fell behind
again. They caught up at about one in the afternoon, carrying
another deer, also shot by Ricardo. Joaquín arrived with them. An
incident was provoked by a slanging match between Joaquín and
el Rubio, and I had to speak to the latter without being convinced
that he was guilty.

I decided anyhow to reach the stream, but we saw a small
aeroplane circling above up to no good, and besides I was worried
because there was no news from the base. I had expected this stage
to take longer, but in spite of the men's weariness, we arrived
at five-thirty in the afternoon. There we were greeted by the
Peruvian doctor, el Negro, who has come with el Chino and the radio
operator; he reported that Benigno was waiting for us with some
food, that two of Moisés Guevara's men have deserted, and that the
police have been to the farm. Benigno explained that he had gone to
meet us with food and had come across Rolando three days ago. He
had stayed here for two days because he did not think it a good
idea to go on, as the army could advance down the river and the
little plane had been circling overhead for the past three days. El
Negro had personally seen the attack on the farm by six men.
Antonio and Coco weren't there; Coco had gone to Camiri to look
for another group of Moisés Guevara's men, and Antonio had left

at once to report the desertions. I received a long message from
Marcos (Document VIII); in it, he explains his actions in his own
way. He went to the farm against my express orders. There were
also two reports from Antonio to explain the situation (Documents
IX and X).

At the base now are the Frenchman, el Chino, his comrades, el
Pelado, Tania and Moisés Guevara with the first part of his group.
After eating a feast of rice and beans with venison, Miguel went out
to look for Joaquín who hadn't arrived and to locate Chinchu, who
had dropped back once more. He returned with Ricardo, and
Joaquín turned up by dawn. We are all grouped here.

MARCH 20

We left at ten o'clock, keeping up a good pace. Benigno and el Negro
went ahead with a message for Marcos; in it, I ordered him to look
after defence matters and to leave administrative questions to
Antonio. Joaquín left at his leisure after covering over our tracks at
the entrance to the creek. Three of his men are barefoot. At one,
during a long halt, Pacho appeared with a message from Marcos.
His report confirmed the first message from Benigno, but the situation
was more complicated now, as 60 soldiers had got onto the trail
of the hunter from Vallegrande and had captured one of our
messengers, Salustio, from Moisés Guevara's group. They had
taken a mule and the jeep was lost. There was no news from el
Loro, who had stayed on guard at the shack. We decided anyway to
reach the Bear Camp, as we call it now, because we killed a bear
there. We sent on Miguel and Urbano to prepare a meal for hungry
men, and we arrived in the evening. Dantón,[1] el Pelao and el Chino
were in the camp, as well as Tania and a Bolivian group used as a
supply unit to bring food and then withdraw. Rolando had been
sent to organize a complete retreat; a climate of defeat prevailed.
Shortly afterwards, a recently-recruited Bolivian doctor arrived with
a message for Rolando, saying that Marcos and Antonio were waiting
at the watering place and wanted to meet him there. I used the same
messenger to tell them that wars are won with bullets, that they should
withdraw at once to the camp, and that they should wait for me
there. There is a terrible impression of total chaos; they do not know
what to do.

I had a preliminary talk with el Chino. He wants 5,000

---

[1] Régis Debray.

dollars a month for ten months, and Havana has told him to talk
it over with me. He also brought a message that Arturo could not
decode because it was so long. I said that I agreed in principle, but
they must start fighting within the next six months. He thinks he can
manage with fifteen men under his command in the Ayacucho
area. We also agreed that he would take five men with him now
and fifteen more later; they would be sent armed and trained for
combat. He must send me a couple of medium-range (40-mile)
transmitters, and we will work out a code for our use to keep in
contact all the time. He seems very enthusiastic about it.

He also brought along a series of reports from Rodolfo, already
completely out of date. We know that el Loro turned up announcing
that he had killed a soldier.

MARCH 21

I spent the day chatting and clearing up some points with el Chino,
the Frenchman, el Pelao and Tania. The Frenchman brought along
stale news about Monje, Simón Reyes, *etc*. He came to stay
with us, but I asked him to go back to France to organize a network
to help us from there; on his way, he could go to Cuba, which would
coincide with his wish to get married and have a son by his comrade.
I must write letters to Sartre and Bertrand Russell, so they can organize
an international fund to raise money for the Bolivian liberation
movement. He must also speak with a friend who will organize ways
to help us, basically money, medicine and electronic equipment,
supplemented by an engineer to set it up.

El Pelao, of course, is willing to serve under my command, and I
proposed that at present he should act as a kind of co-ordinator with
the groups under Jozamy, Gelman and Stamponi, and that he should
send me five men to begin training. He will give my regards to María
Rosa Oliver and to my father. He will be given 500 pesos to send off
and 1,000 for his travels. If they accept, they should begin to explore
in the north of Argentina and send me a report.

Tania made the contacts and the people came, but according to her,
they made her travel in their jeep as far as here; she was planning
to stay for one day, but things became complicated. Jozamy could
not stay the first time and he did not even contact us the second time
because Tania was here. She refers to Iván with some contempt; I do
not know what is at the bottom of all this. Loyola's account up till the

65

9th of February (1,500 dollars) was submitted[1].

We also received two reports from Iván; one of little interest with photographs of a military academy; another giving us various details, also of little importance.

The basic problem is that we cannot decipher the writing (Document XIII). We received a report from Antonio (Document XII) trying to justify his attitude. We heard a radio message which announced a death, later denied; this indicates that el Loro's story is true.

MARCH 22

At [   ][2] we left, abandoning the camp [   ] with some food, poorly stored [   ]. We got down below at noon. We form a party of forty-seven men, including our visitors and everyone.

When we arrived Inti pointed out a whole lot of ways in which Marcos had lacked consideration. I exploded and told Marcos that we would certainly have to expel him from the guerrilla. He answered that he would rather we shot him.

We sent five men to set an ambush further ahead along the river and three men to explore; Antonio was the leader with Miguel and el Loro. Pacho went to keep watch from the barren hill overlooking Argañaraz's house, but he didn't spot anything. The explorers came back at night, and I gave them a severe reprimand. Olo reacted in a very emotional way and denied my charges. The meeting was explosive and tempestuous and did not go well. It is not yet clear what Marcos said. I sent for Rolando to settle the question of the numbers and distribution of the new recruits once and for all, because there were already 30 men in the centre party going hungry.

MARCH 23

A day of real war. Pombo wanted to organize a supply expedition up to the top to rescue some provisions, but I opposed this until the situation with Marcos had been settled. At about eight o'clock, Coco came rushing over to report that a section of the army had fallen into the ambush. The result up till now is three 60mm mortars, sixteen Mausers, two Bz, three USIS, one .30, two radios, boots, *etc.*, seven killed, four wounded and fourteen unwounded prisoners; but we were unable to capture their food supplies. Their plan of operations was

---

1 She also reported that she was no longer the leader of the [Communist] Youth.
2 The blank spaces correspond to illegible words in the original text.

captured; it consisted of an advance from both ends of the Nacahuasu to make contact at its middle point. We rapidly moved the men to the other side and placed Marcos with almost the whole of the advance party at the end of the road we use for manœuvres, while the centre and some of the rear party stayed on the defensive and Braulio set an ambush at the end of the other road for manœuvres. We will spend the night like this, waiting for tomorrow to see if the famous Rangers turn up. The captured major and captain talked like parrots.

We are decoding the message sent with el Chino. It speaks of Debray's journey and the remittance of the $60,000 wanted by el Chino, and it explains why they are not writing to Iván. I also received a message from Sánchez where he reports on the possibilities of establishing Mito at certain points.

MARCH 24

The full booty is as follows : sixteen Mausers, three mortars with 64 bombs, two Bz, 2,000 rounds of Mauser ammunition, three USIS with two clips each, one .30 with two belts of ammunition. There are seven dead, four wounded and fourteen prisoners. We sent Marcos out to scout, but he did not find out anything, except that the aeroplanes are bombing near our house.

I sent Inti to talk with the prisoners for the last time and to free them, after stripping them of everything we could use. The officers were spoken to separately and left with their possessions. We told the major that we would give him until noon on the 27th to take away the dead and we offered them a truce in the whole Lagunillas area if he stayed near there, but he replied that he was retiring from the army. The captain told us that he had rejoined the army a year ago, because people in the Party had asked him to do so, and that he had a brother studying in Cuba; he also gave us the names of two other officers who would be willing to collaborate with us. When the aeroplanes began bombing, it made them panic suddenly; but it also had the same effect on two of our own men, Raúl and Walter. Walter was also rather feeble in the ambush.

Marcos went out scouting without finding anything in his area. Nato and Coco went with the worst of the men on a supply expedition to the top, but these men had to be brought back because they refused to march. They must be discharged.

MARCH 25

Nothing new happened today. León, Urbano and Arturo were sent

67

to a look-out which dominates both accesses to the river. At noon, Marcos withdrew from his position in ambush and everybody stayed concentrated on the main ambush. At 18 : 30, in front of nearly all the group, I made an analysis of our expedition and its significance. I exposed the mistakes made by Marcos and took away his command. I then named Miguel as chief of the advance party, and announced at the same time that Paco, Pepe, Chingolo, and Eusebio were discharged, telling them that they would not eat if they did not work, suspending their supply of cigarettes, and redistributing their personal things among the most needy of the comrades. I referred to Kolle's project to come here and discuss what is to be done simultaneously with the expulsion from the Communist Youth of those members present with us. The facts matter here; words that don't coincide with facts are unimportant. I announced a search for the cow and a re-opening of our studies.

I spoke with Pedro and the Doctor, and I announced to them that they had almost fully graduated as guerrilla fighters, and I encouraged Apolinar along with them. I criticized Walter for weakening during the expedition, for his attitude in combat and for his fear during the bombardment. He did not react well. We cleared up various details with el Chino and el Pelado and I made a long oral report on the situation to the Frenchman. During the course of the meeting, the group was given the name of the National Liberation Army of Bolivia and a report will be made of the skirmish.

MARCH 26

Inti left early with Antonio, Raúl and Pedro to look for a cow in the Ticucha area, but they met troops three hours away from here and came back, apparently without being seen. They reported that the soldiers have a look-out on a bare hill and another in a house with a shiny roof, from which eight men were seen leaving. They are in the neighbourhood of the river we used to call the Yaqui. I spoke with Marcos and I sent him to the rear party; I do not think that his conduct will improve much.

We sent out a small supply expedition and the usual guards. From the look-out at Argañaraz's, 30 to 40 soldiers were spotted and a helicopter landed.

MARCH 27

The news broke today, taking over most of the programmes on the radio and producing a host of *communiqués,* including a press conference by Barrientos. The official report gave one more death than our figures did, and claimed that they were wounded and then shot. It claims that we have fifteen dead and four taken prisoner, two of whom are foreigners. They also speak of a foreigner who committed suicide and of the composition of the guerrilla. It is obvious that the deserters or the prisoner talked, but we do not know how much they said and how it was put. Everything seems to indicate that Tania has been identified, which means that two years of good and patient work are lost. It is very difficult for people now to leave the area. I got the impression that Dantón did not like it at all when I told him so. We shall see in the future.

Benigno, el Loro and Julio went out to look for the road to Pirirenda; it will take them two or three days and they are instructed not to be seen in Pirirenda so that they can go on a later expedition to Gutiérrez. The reconnaissance aircraft dropped some parachutes which the look-out reported had fallen in our hunting-ground. We sent Antonio and two others out to investigate and to try and take prisoners, but they did not get anything.

In the evening we had a staff meeting in which we worked out our plans for the future. Tomorrow, a supply expedition will be sent to our little house to collect some maize, and later another will go to buy things in Gutiérrez, and finally a small diversionary attack is planned to take place, perhaps in the forest on the vehicles which pass between Pincal and Lagunillas.

We composed our *Communiqué* No. 1, which we will try to get to the journalists in Camiri (Document XVII).

MARCH 28

The radio is still full of news about the guerrillas. We are surrounded by 2,000 men within a radius of 120 kilometres, and the circle is closing in, backed by napalm air raids. We are said to have about ten to fifteen casualties.

I sent Braulio with nine men to try to find some maize. They came back at night with a whole lot of crazy news : 1) Coco, who had gone ahead to give us warning, had disappeared. 2) At four o'clock when they reached the farm, they found that the cave had been searched. They fanned out to begin withdrawing when seven men from the Red Cross, two doctors and several unarmed soldiers appeared. They were captured, were told that the truce was over, and yet allowed to carry on. 3) A lorry-load of soldiers arrived, and, instead of shooting at them,

69

our men got them to agree to withdraw. 4) The soldiers
retreated in good order and our men took the medical people to where
the decomposing corpses lay, but they couldn't carry them away and
said they would come back tomorrow to burn them. They confiscated
two of Argañaraz's horses and went back, leaving Antonio, el Rubio
and Aniceto in a place where the animals could not follow them any
further. As they were looking for Coco, he appeared; apparently, he
had remained asleep.

There is no news about Benigno yet.

The Frenchman was somewhat too eloquent when he described how
useful he could be outside.

MARCH 29

Day of little action, but of extraordinary happenings on the news : the
army is letting out a lot of information, which can be of great
value to us if it is true. Radio Havana has broadcast the news already
and the government announces that it will back Venezuela's action
in presenting the Cuban case to the Organization of American States.
There was one bit of news which worried me; there has been a
skirmish in the Tiraboy ravine where two guerrilla fighters were
killed. This is on the way to Pirirenda, the place where Benigno was
told to scout; he was due back today, but he hasn't turned up.
He was ordered not to go through the ravine, but in these last few
days the orders I give have been repeatedly disobeyed.

Moisés Guevara is progressing very slowly with his work; he was
given some dynamite, but they were unable to explode it all day.
A horse was killed and a lot of its meat was eaten, although it has to
last for four days; we will try to bring the other one as far as here,
but it will be difficult. Judging by the birds of prey, the bodies have
not been burned yet. As soon as the cave is finished, we can transfer
from this camp, which is becoming uncomfortable and too well
known. I informed Alejandro that he will stay here with the doctor
and Joaquín (probably in the Bear Camp). Rolando is also extremely
exhausted.

I talked with Urbano and Tuma; I could not even make Tuma
understand the origins of my criticism.

MARCH 30

Everything is quiet once again : Benigno and his comrades arrived by
the middle of the morning. In fact, they had gone through the Tiraboy
ravine, but they only found the tracks of two other people. Although

70

they were spotted by the peasants, they reached their destination and returned. Their report states that it takes about four hours to get to Pirirenda and that, apparently, there is no danger. The air force constantly machine-gunned the little house.

I sent Antonio and two others to explore upriver and they report that the soldiers remain static, although there are signs of a patrol along the river. Trenches have been dug.

We have got the mare that was missing, so that we have meat for four days, if the worst comes to the worst. We will rest tomorrow, and the day after tomorrow the advance party will leave on the next two operations: to take Gutiérrez and to lay an ambush on the road between Argañaraz's and Lagunillas.

MARCH 31

No major news. Moisés Guevara announced that the cave would be completed tomorrow. Inti and Ricardo reported that the soldiers had again taken our little farm, after an artillery barrage (mortars), air raids, *etc*. This obstructed our plans to go to Pirirenda for supplies; nevertheless, I instructed Manuel to advance to the little house with his men. If it is empty, he is to take it and to let me know so that we can get moving the day after tomorrow; if it is taken and a surprise attack cannot be carried out, he is to return and consider the possibility of outflanking Argañaraz's to lay an ambush between Pincal and Lagunillas. The radio continues its nattering, and news dispatches are followed by official announcements of fighting. They have fixed our position very precisely between the Yaqui and the Nacahuasu, and I fear they will make some effort to encircle us. I talked with Benigno about his mistake in not going to look for us and I explained to him Marcos's situation. His reaction was good.

During the night, I spoke with el Loro and Aniceto. The conversation went very badly. El Loro even said that we were breaking up, and when I asked him what he meant, he left it to Marcos and Benigno to explain. Aniceto went halfway with him, but later he confessed to Coco that they had been accomplices in stealing some tins and to Inti that he did not go along with el Loro about Benigno nor with somebody else about Pombo nor about " the general deterioration of the guerrilla," or something like that.

ANALYSIS OF THE MONTH

The month was full of events, but the general outlook has the following characteristics: a stage of purification and consolidation for

71

*the guerrilla, fully carried out; a slow stage of development with the
incorporation of some Cuban elements, who do not seem bad, and
of Moisés Guevara's men, who turned out to be very substandard
(two deserters, one prisoner who ' squealed ', three expelled, two
feeble); a stage of the start of the fight, characterized by a precise and
spectacular attack, but full of clumsy and indecisive actions before and
afterwards (Marcos's retreat, Braulio's action); a stage of the start
of the enemy's counter-offensive, characterized up till now by: (a) a
tendency to establish controls that may isolate us; (b) a clamouring
at a national and an international level; (c) total ineffectiveness up
till now; (d) mobilization of the peasants.*

*Evidently, we will have to start the march sooner than I thought
and get a move on, leaving a group in reserve, and with the
handicap of four possible informers. The situation is not good, but
another stage of testing now begins for the guerrilla, which will do
the men a lot of good when they have got through it.*

*Composition of the advance party—Commander: Miguel.
Benigno, Pacho, Loro, Aniceto, Camba, Coco, Darío, Julio, Pablo,
Raúl.*

*The rear party—Commander: Joaquín. Second: Braulio. Rubio,
Marcos, Pedro, the Doctor, Polo, Walter, Victor (Pepe, Paco,
Eusebio, Chingolo).*

*The centre party—myself, Alejandro, Rolando, Inti, Pombo,
Nato, Tuma, Urbano, Moro, Negro, Ricardo, Arturo, Eustaquio,
Moisés Guevara, Willy, Luis[1], Antonio, León (Tania, Pelado, Dantón,
el Chino—visitors), (Serapio—refugee).*

APRIL, 1967

APRIL 1

The advance party left at seven in the morning, rather behind time.
Camba is missing. He hasn't returned from his expedition with el Nato
to hide the weapons in the Bear cave. At ten Tuma arrived from
the look-out, reporting that he had seen three or four soldiers in our
little hunting field. We took up our posts and Walter warned us from
his look-out that he had seen three soldiers with a mule or a donkey,
and that they were putting something in position; he pointed it out
to me, but I didn't see anything. I withdrew at four in the afternoon,
judging that it was unnecessary to remain there in any case

---

[1] Also appears later as Chapaco.

72

because they would not attack. I think the whole thing was Walter's optical illusion.

I decided to evacuate everything tomorrow and to put Rolando in charge of the rear party while Joaquín was absent. El Nato and Camba arrived at 22 : 00, after hiding everything except for a meal for the six men who were to stay there. These are : Joaquín, Alejandro, Moro, Serapio, Eustaquio and Polo. The three Cubans protested. We killed the other mare, to leave *charqui*[1] for the six men. At eleven at night, Antonio arrived with a sack of maize and the news that everything had gone smoothly.

At four in the morning, Rolando left, taking with him the handicap of the four feeble ones (Chingolo, Eusebio, Paco, Pepe). Pepe wanted to be given a gun and to stay. Camba went with him.

At five, Coco arrived with a new message stating that a cow had been slaughtered and that they were waiting for us. I fixed a rendezvous at noon the day after tomorrow at the stream, which comes out of the forest below the farm.

APRIL 2

The incredible amount of things that had accumulated, forced us to spend the whole day storing them in their respective caves; the transfer wasn't over until five in the afternoon. A watch of four men was kept up, but the day went by in a dead calm; no aeroplanes flew over the area. The commentaries on the radio spoke of " narrowing the circle " and of the guerrilla fighters readying themselves for the defence of the Nacahuasu pass; they announced the arrest of Don Remberto and described how he sold the farm to Coco.

As time was getting on, we decided not to set out today, but at three o'clock tomorrow morning; we would gain an entire day by going directly along the Nacahuasu, even though our rendezvous is the other way. I spoke with Moro, explaining to him that I had not put him among the best men because he had certain weaknesses over food and a tendency to annoy the comrades with his jokes. We talked for a while on these topics.

APRIL 3

Our programme was carried out without problems; we left at 3 : 30 and travelled slowly until we passed the bend of the short cut at 6 : 30 and reached the limits of the farm at 8 : 30. When

---

[1] *Charqui* : Meat dried in the sun and salted.

we went through the place where the ambush had been set, nothing
was left of the corpses except the skeletons, picked perfectly
clean; the birds of prey had done their duty with great
thoroughness. I sent two men (Urbano and Nato) to make contact
with Rolando, and we moved on during the afternoon to the Tiraboy
ravine where we slept, stuffed with beef and maize.

I spoke with Dantón and Carlos, giving them three alternatives:
to stay with us, to go off alone, or to go to take Gutiérrez and try
their luck from there as best they could. They chose the third. We
will try our luck tomorrow.

APRIL 6

Day of great tension. We crossed the Nacahuasu river at four in the
morning and waited for daylight before continuing; later, Miguel
began to scout, but he had to come back twice because of his
mistakes which put us very close to the soldiers. At eight, Rolando
reported that there were about ten soldiers in front of the ravine
that we had just evacuated. We left slowly and at eleven we were
already on a wooded ridge out of danger. Rolando arrived with the
news that there had been more than a hundred soldiers posted in the
ravine.

In the night, when we hadn't yet reached the stream, cowherds'
voices were heard from the river. We emerged and captured four
peasants who had some of Argañaraz's cows with them. They had a
safe-conduct from the army to look for twelve stray cattle; some had
already wandered off and were impossible to find. We kept two cows
for ourselves and we drove them along the river to our stream.
The four civilians turned out to be the contractor and his son,
a peasant from Chuquisaca and another from Camiri, who seemed
to be very well-disposed and promised to circulate the document
which we gave him.

We held them for a while and then we released them, asking them
to keep their mouths shut, which they promised to do.

We spent the night eating.

APRIL 7

We pushed far up the stream, driving the surviving cow, which
we then slaughtered to make *charqui*. Rolando stayed in ambush
on the river with orders to shoot at anything that appeared;
nothing showed up all day. Benigno and Camba went on with the
track that was to take us to Pirirenda, and they reported that they

74

had heard something like the motor of a sawmill in a canyon near our stream.

I sent Urbano and Julio with a message for Joaquín and they have not returned today.

Nothing much happened today. Benigno went and came back from his work without finishing it and declared that it wouldn't be finished by tomorrow either. Miguel left to look for the canyon which Benigno saw from the top and did not return. Urbano and Julio came back with Polo. The soldiers have taken the camp and are sending out reconnaissance parties on the hills; they passed our hoist coming down from the top. Joaquín reports these and other problems in the enclosed Document XIX.

We had three cows with their calves, but one lot escaped, leaving us with four animals. With the salt we still have, we will make *charqui* out of one or two of them.

APRIL 9

Polo, Luis and Willy went on a mission to take a note to Joaquín and to help them come back to position themselves in some hiding place upstream, which Nato and Moisés Guevara will select. According to Nato, there are some good places a little more than an hour from here, only rather too near the stream. Miguel came back from his scouting; the canyon comes out at Pirirenda and will take a day's march with rucksacks. So I told Benigno to stop making his way through, as this would take at least one more day.

APRIL 10

Dawn and morning passed uneventfully as we got ready to leave the unpolluted stream and cross by Miguel's canyon to Pirirenda-Gutiérrez. In the middle of the morning, el Negro arrived, very agitated. He announced that fifteen soldiers were coming downriver. Inti had gone to warn Rolando in the ambush. We could not do anything else but wait, and this we did; I sent Tuma off so that he could be ready to report to me. Soon we had the first bad news: el Rubio, Jesús Suárez Gayol, had been mortally wounded. He had died from a bullet in the head by the time they brought him back to the camp. It happened like this: the ambush was set up by eight men from the rear party—reinforced by three from the advance party, distributed on both banks of the river. When the arrival

75

of the fifteen soldiers was reported, Inti passed el Rubio's position
and observed that he was in a very bad spot, since he was clearly
visible from the river. The soldiers advanced without taking much
care, but they were searching the banks for our tracks, and while
doing this, they ran straight into Braulio or Pedro before falling
into the ambush. The shooting lasted a few seconds, leaving on the
ground one dead man and three wounded and six more prisoners;
a little later, a sub-lieutenant also fell and four soldiers escaped.
El Rubio, already in agony, was found by the side of a wounded
soldier; his Garand was jammed and an unexploded grenade with its
pin loose was by his side. The wounded man could not be interrogated
due to his critical condition; he died a little later as did the
sub-lieutenant in command of them.

The interrogation of the prisoners built up the following picture :
these fifteen men belong to the same company that was up the
Nacahuasu river. They had come through the canyon, collected
the remains, and then had taken the camp. According to the
soldiers, they had not discovered anything, although the radio
talks of documents and photographs found there. The company
is made up of a hundred men; fifteen of them went to escort
a group of journalists to our camp, and the rest had gone on scouting
missions with orders to return by five o'clock. The larger forces are
at Pincal; there are some 30 soldiers in Lagunillas, and the
group that was seen in the Tiraboy ravine has supposedly retreated
to Gutiérrez. They told us the odyssey of his group lost in the
woods without water; they had had to be rescued. I calculated
that the escaped soldiers would get back to their lines late, so I
decided to leave the ambush where it was, as Rolando had already
advanced some 500 metres with the help now of all the
advance party. At first I had ordered their retreat, but then I thought
it logic to leave them as they were. At about 17 :00, the news came
that the army was advancing with a large number of troops.
Nothing to do except wait. I sent Pombo to get a clear
picture of the situation. We listened to isolated shots for a while,
and then Pombo came back to say the soldiers had fallen into the
ambush again; several were dead and a major captured.

This time, things went as follows : they fanned out to advance
along the river, but they took no precautions and the surprise was
total. This time there were seven dead, five wounded and a total of
22 prisoners. The final result is the following : (total). (I
cannot give this because of the lack of data).

In the morning, we began to transfer all our belongings and we
buried el Rubio in a small grave near the surface, owing to the
lack of materials. We left Inti with the rear party to escort the
prisoners and to set them free, also to bring back any weapons lying
around. The only result of the search was to take two more prisoners,
both carrying Garands. The two parts of Report No. 1 were handed
to the major, who promised that he would give them to the press.
Total losses worked out as follows : ten dead, including two
lieutenants; 30 prisoners, including a major and some lesser
officers, the rest soldiers; six were wounded, one in the first fight
and five in the second. They are under the command of the 4th
Division, but elements from other regiments are with them;
there are Rangers, paratroopers, and local soldiers who are almost
children.

We did not finish transporting things until the afternoon and we
found a cave in which to leave our equipment, although we didn't
prepare it properly. During the last stage, the cows were scared and
escaped, leaving us only with a calf, nothing more.

Early, just as we reached the new camp, we met Joaquín and
Alejandro, who were coming down with all their men. Their
report showed that the soldiers seen by Eustaquio were only a
fantasy of his, and that our transfer up to here was a useless effort.

The radio reported ' a new and bloody clash ' and spoke of nine
dead soldiers and four ' confirmed ' dead on our side.

A Chilean reporter gave a detailed description of our camp and
discovered a photograph of me without a beard and with a pipe.
We will have to make more investigations about how he got it.
There is no proof that the upper cave has been located, although
there are some signs that it has been.

At six-thirty in the morning, I brought together all the combatants
except for the four who were in disgrace; we paid homage to el
Rubio and pointed out that the first blood to be spilled was Cuban.
I brought up a matter I have noticed in the advance party, which
is the tendency to downgrade the Cubans; this came to a head
yesterday when el Camba said that every day he had less
confidence in the Cubans, in the course of an argument with
Ricardo. I made a new appeal for unity as the only way to develop
our army, which increases its fire power and combat experience, but

77

does not grow in numbers; on the contrary, it has diminished lately.

After hiding our spoils in a cave well-prepared by el Nato, we left at two in the afternoon, at a slow pace, so slow that we hardly advanced, and slept at a small watering place near where we had started.

The army now admits to eleven dead; apparently, another body has been found or one of the wounded has died. I started giving a brief course on Debray's book.

We have deciphered a bit of the message, which does not seem very important.

APRIL 13

We split up the group into two halves, so that we can travel more rapidly; in spite of everything, we progressed slowly, reaching our camp at 16 :00 and the stragglers at 18 :30. Miguel had got there in the morning; the caves have not been discovered and nothing has been touched; the benches, the stoves, the oven and the seedbags are intact.

Aniceto and Raúl went out to explore, but they did not do it well and must persist in it tomorrow as far as the Iquiri river.

The North Americans have announced that the military advisers sent to Bolivia were part of an old plan and had nothing to do with the guerrillas. Perhaps we are present at the first episode in a new Vietnam.

APRIL 14

Monotonous day. We brought some supplies from the shelter for the wounded; this gives us enough food for five days. From the upper cave we took the tins of milk and discovered that 23 of them were missing; this is inexplicable, as Moro left 48 and nobody seems to have had the time to take them. Tinned milk is a great corrupter. We took a mortar and a machine-gun out of the special cave to reinforce our position until Joaquín comes. Our tactics for the operation are not clear, but I think that the best plan is for everybody to go out and operate in the Muyupampa zone, then to retreat to the north. If possible, Dantón and Carlos will be left on their route towards Sucre-Cochabamba, depending on the circumstances. Message No. 2 (Document XXI) was written for the Bolivian people and Report No. 4 for Manila, which should be delivered by the Frenchman.

Joaquín arrived with all the rear party and we decided to leave
tomorrow. He reported that there had been flights over the zone
and that they had used a cannon to fire into the woods. The day
passed without anything happening. The arming of the group was
completed; the .30 machine-gun was assigned to the rear party
(Marcos) with the ones in disgrace to help him.

At night, I gave a talk about our route and about the disappearance
of the tins of milk, giving a severe warning about this.

We decoded part of a long message from Cuba. To sum it up,
Lechín knows about my plans and is going to write a declaration
supporting us; he will re-enter the country clandestinely within twenty
days.

I wrote a note to Fidel (# 4) reporting the recent events. It is coded
and written in invisible ink.

The advance party left at 6 : 15 and we left at 7 : 15,
travelling well until the Iquiri river, but Tania and Alejandro fell
behind. When we took their temperature, Tania's was 39° C and
Alejandro's 38° C. In addition, the delay prevented us from travelling
according to schedule. We left the two of them with el Negro and
Serapio one kilometre up the Iquiri river and we went on, going by
a hamlet called Bella Vista, which contains all of four peasants,
who sold us potatoes, a pig and some maize. They are poor peasants
and they are terrorized by our presence here. We spent the night
cooking and eating and we didn't move, waiting for tomorrow night
to go to Ticucha without being noticed because of our characteristics.

The news was variable and so were our decisions : Ticucha is a waste
of time, according to the peasants, as there is a road straight to
Muyupampa (Vaca Guzmán) which is shorter and allows vehicles
to get through on its last stretch. We decided to continue straight to
Muyupampa after many hesitations on my part. I sent somebody to
tell the four stragglers to stay with Joaquín and to give him orders
to make a show of strength in the zone so as to keep down the
enemy's mobility. He was to wait for us for three days; after that, he
was to remain in the zone without any head-on fighting and wait for
our return. At night, we learned that one of the peasant's sons had
disappeared and might have gone to warn the troops, but in spite
of this we decided to leave, so as to get rid of the Frenchman and

Carlos once and for all. Moisés joined the group of stragglers; he had to stay behind with a bad attack in his gall bladder.

Here is the plan of our situation :

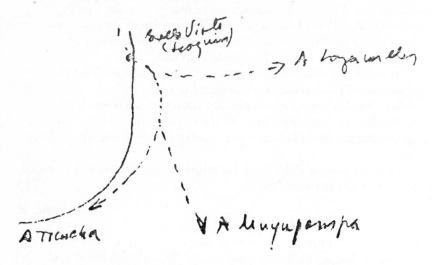

If we take the same way back, we expose ourselves to a clash with the army on the alert in Lagunillas or a column coming from Ticucha, but we must do it so we don't get cut off from the rear party.

We left at 22 :00, travelling at intervals until 4 :30, when we halted for a bit of sleep. We advanced some ten kilometres. Out of all the peasants we met, only one, Simón, showed himself to be co-operative, although frightened. Another one, Vides, can be dangerous; he is the " rich one " of the area. We also have to consider the missing son of Carlos Rodas who might well be a little scoundrel (though under the thumb of Vides, who is the boss economically of the area).

APRIL 18

We travelled until early morning, drowsy during the last hour of the night and really feeling the cold. The advance party went to scout in the morning and found the house of some Guaraní Indians who gave them very little information. Our sentries stopped a horseman who turned out to be another son of Carlos Rodas; he was going to Yakunday and we took him prisoner. We travelled slowly and, at 3 :00, we arrived at Matagal, at the house of A. Padilla, the poor brother of another man who lives a league away from here and whose house we passed. The man was scared and used every means

80

to convince us to leave, but to top it all, it started to rain and we had
to take shelter in his house.

We remained in the area all day, detaining the peasants who came to
the crossing from both directions, so that we had a surfeit of
prisoners. At 13 : 00 the sentry brought a Trojan Horse : an English
journalist called Roth, who was led here by some children from
Lagunillas following our tracks. His papers were in order, but certain
things about him were suspicious. In his passport, the word ' student '
was crossed and changed to ' journalist ' (he says he is in fact a
photographer); he had a visa to Puerto Rico and then when
questioned about a postcard from a Peace Corps organizer in Buenos
Aires, he confessed to being a Spanish teacher for the U.S. Peace
Corpsmen there. He said that he had been to our camp and he had
been shown a diary of Braulio's, where he told of his experiences
and travels. It is always the same story. Indiscipline and
irresponsibility directing all. Reports from the little boys who guided
the journalist told us that our arrival here was known that same night
in Lagunillas, thanks to information brought by somebody. We put
pressure on Rodas's son and he confessed that his brother and
one of Vides's peons had gone to win the reward of $500 to $1,000
for us. We confiscated his horse as a reprisal and we told this to
the peasants we had detained.
    The Frenchman asked if he could talk things over with the
Englishman, who was to prove his good faith by helping him and
Carlos to get out. Carlos accepted this reluctantly, and I washed my
hands of it. We arrived at 21 : 00 at [   ] and
went on our way towards Muyupampa, where, according to the
peasants' reports, everything was quiet. The Englishman accepted
the conditions put to him by Inti, which included taking a short
message written by me. At 23 : 45, after shaking hands with those
who were leaving, the march to take the town began. I stayed behind
with Pombo, Tuma and Urbano. It was exceedingly cold and we made
a small fire. At 1:00, el Nato came to report that the town was in a
state of alert with twenty armed troops quartered there and defensive
patrols. One of these, with two M-3s and two revolvers, surprised
our forward men, but surrendered without a fight. I was asked for
instructions and I told them to withdraw as it was so late, leaving
the English journalist, the Frenchman and Carlos to do whatever
suited them. At 4:00 we began our retreat, without having achieved

our objective; but Carlos decided to stay behind and the Frenchman followed him, this time unwillingly.

We arrived at about 7:00, at Nemesio Caraballo's house; we had met him during the night and he had invited us to coffee. The man had gone, locking the house and only leaving some scared servants behind. We organized a meal for ourselves there, buying maize and squash from the peons. At about 13:00 a small lorry with a white flag drove up, bringing the sub-prefect, the doctor and the priest (who is German) from Muyupampa. Inti talked with them. They had come for peace, but for a national peace, with them in the role of intermediaries. Inti offered them peace for Muyupampa on condition they returned with a list of supplies before 18:30. They did not commit themselves to do this, because the army, according to them, was in control of the town. They asked us to extend the time until 6:00 next morning, but we did not accept this.

As a sign of goodwill, they had brought two cartons of cigarettes and the news that the three who tried to get away had been captured in Muyupampa and that two of them were compromised by having forged papers. Things look bad for Carlos: Dantón should get out all right.

At 17:30 three AT-6s came and bombed the very house where we were cooking. One of the bombs fell fifteen metres away and slightly wounded Ricardo with a piece of shrapnel. This was the army's answer. We must find out their proclamations so we can demoralize their soldiers thoroughly. Judging by the ones sent out against us, they're scared out of their wits.

We left at 22:30, with two horses, the one we confiscated and the journalist's. We travelled towards Ticucha until 1:30, when we halted to sleep.

We travelled a short distance to reach the house of Rosa Carrasco, who looked after us very well, selling us what we needed. We travelled by night until the cross-roads on the Muyupampa-Monteagudo highway, to a place called Taperillas. The idea was to stay at a watering place and to make a scouting trip to find somewhere for an ambush. There was another reason, a radio announcement of the death of three mercenaries, a Frenchman, an Englishman and an Argentinian. We have to establish if this is true or not; if it is, we must teach them a good lesson.

Before dinner we went to the house of the veteran Rodas, the step-father of Vargas, who died at the Nacahuasu. We gave him an explanation, which seemed to satisfy him. The advance party did not understand properly and went on, waking some dogs who barked extremely loudly.

APRIL 22

The mistakes began in the morning. Rolando, Miguel and Antonio went to search for a place to lay an ambush after we had withdrawn deep into the forest, but they surprised some men from a small YPFB truck analyzing our footprints while a peasant was telling them about our passing in the night. Our men decided to take everybody prisoner. This dislocated our plans, but we decided to lay an ambush during the day and capture the passing supply trucks and ambush the army if it came. A truck with some goods and a lot of bananas and a load of peasants was seized, but another one coming through to examine our footprints was allowed to pass, and, to top it all, so were other small trucks from the oil company. The food, combined with the temptation of bread that was offered and never arrived, kept us delayed there.

I intended to load the oil company's small truck with all the foodstuffs and progress with the advance party as far as the cross-roads at Ticucha, situated four kilometres away. In the evening, a small aeroplane began to circle over our position and the barking of the dogs in the nearby houses became more insistent. At 20 : 00, we were ready to leave in spite of the evidence that our presence had been detected, when a short combat began and we heard voices demanding our surrender. All of us were taken by surprise and I had no idea what was happening. Fortunately, our belongings and the goods were in the little truck. A little while later, things got organized; only el Loro was missing, but all the signs were that he was safe for the time being, because the shooting had begun with Ricardo surprising the guide of the soldiers who were climbing the ridge to encircle us. The guide may have been wounded.

We left with the small truck and the available horses, six in all; the men sometimes walked and sometimes rode, ending with an advance guard of six horsemen and the rest in the small truck. We got to Ticucha at 3:30, and to el Mesón, the priest's property, at 6 :30, after getting stuck in a hole.

In balance, the action was negative; bad discipline and bad

planning on the one hand, and the loss of a man (although I hope it is only temporary) on the other. Merchandise which we paid for and did not receive, and, to crown it all, the loss of a wad of dollars which fell out of Pombo's pocket. Not counting the fact that we were taken by surprise and forced to retire by a group which must certainly have been small. We still have a long way to go before we turn this into a combat force, although morale is quite high.

APRIL 23

A day of rest was announced and passed uneventfully. At mid-day, the small plane (AT-6) flew over the area; we reinforced the guard, but nothing happened. The instructions for tomorrow were given at night. Benigno and Aniceto will go and look for Joaquín for four days; Coco and Camba will explore the track to the Grande river and will prepare a proper path for the next four days; we will stay here near the maize, waiting to see if the army comes, until Joaquín can join us. His orders are to bring everyone and only to leave one of the men in disgrace back there, if sick.

What has happened to Dantón, el Pelado and the English journalist still remains a mystery; the press is censored and there has already been another announcement of a clash where three to five prisoners were taken.

APRIL 24

The scouts left. We moved one kilometre upstream onto a little ridge, from where we can keep a look-out as far as the last peasant's house, some 500 metres before the priest's farm (we found marijuana in the fields). The peasant came again and seemed curious; in the afternoon, an AT-6 strafed the little house twice. Pacho has mysteriously disappeared; he was sick and stayed behind. Antonio showed him the way and he marched off in the direction from where he should have arrived within five hours, but he did not come back. We will look for him tomorrow.

APRIL 25

A black day. At about 10 in the morning, Pombo came back from the look-out to tell us that 30 soldiers were advancing on the little house. Antonio stayed in the look-out. While we were getting ready, he arrived with the news that there were 60 men and they were proceeding to advance. The look-out turned out to be inefficient in giving us plenty of advance warning. We decided to plan an improvised ambush in the access road to the camp. Very quickly, we selected a short stretch that bordered the stream with a visibility of 50 metres. I stationed myself there with Urbano and Miguel and the automatic rifle; the Doctor, Arturo and Raúl took up their positions on the right to stop any attempt at flight or advance on that side; Rolando, Pombo, Antonio, Ricardo, Julio, Pablito, Darío, Willy and León occupied the side position on the other bank of the stream, to take the soldiers completely on their flank; Inti stayed in the river bed to attack those who fell back to find refuge there; Nato and Eustaquio went to the look-out with instructions to retreat to the rear when the shooting started; el Chino stayed at the rear, guarding the camp. My scant forces were three men short: Pacho, lost, and Tuma and Luis out looking for him.

A little later, the first soldiers appeared, led to our surprise by three German sheep-dogs with their trainer. The animals were excited, but I did not think they would give us away. They continued advancing, however, and I fired at the first dog, missing it, and when I swung to get the trainer, the M-2 jammed. Miguel killed another dog, as far as I could see, and nobody else came into the ambush. Sporadic firing broke out on the flank of the army. When it stopped for a moment, I sent Urbano to order the retreat, but he came back with the news that Rolando was wounded. They brought him along a little later; he had already lost a lot of blood and was sinking fast. He died when we started to give him plasma. A bullet had fractured his femur and the whole nervous-vascular system; he bled to death before we could do anything. We have lost the best man in the guerrilla, and naturally, one of its pillars; he had been my comrade since he was almost a child, when he was the messenger in Column 4, then onto the invasion and this new revolutionary adventure. I can only say of his obscure death for a hypothetical future which could crystallize: ' *Tu cadáver pequeño de capitán valiente ha extendido en lo inmenso su metálica forma.*'

The rest was the slow process of retreat, salvaging all the things and the body of Rolando (San Luis). Pacho joined us later: he had lost his way and had met Coco, but night caught him on his way back. At 15:00, we buried the body under a thin cover of earth. At 16:00, Benigno and Aniceto came to report that they had fallen into an ambush (or rather a skirmish) with the army; they had lost their rucksacks, but had come out of it unhurt. This happened, according to Benigno's calculations, when they were near the Nacahuasu. Now that both our logical routes are blocked, we will

have to ' take to the hills;' since the exit by the Grande river is not
a good one for two reasons; the first, that it is the natural way to
take, and the second, that it separates us from Joaquín, whom we
have no news from. By night we reached the fork of the roads to the
Nacahuasu and the Grande, and we slept there. We will wait here
for Coco and Camba, to concentrate our little troop. In balance,
the operation was highly negative : Rolando is dead, but not only
that; the maximum losses we inflicted on the army cannot be more
than two men and the dog, since our position was not thought out nor
prepared and our marksmen could not see the enemy. Finally, the
look-out was very badly placed, something which stopped us from
making our preparations in time.

A helicopter landed twice by the priest's house; we do not know
whether a wounded man was removed or not; the air force bombed
our old positions, which means that they have not advanced at all.

APRIL 26

We walked for a few metres and I ordered Miguel to look for a
place to camp, while we sent somebody to search for Coco and Camba,
but he showed up with both of them by noon. According to the two of
them, they had worked to clear four hours' march on the trail under a
heavy load, and there were possibilities for trying to climb the ridge.
Nevertheless, I sent Benigno and Urbano to explore a possible
escalade near the canyon of the stream that flows into the Nacahuasu,
but they came back in the evening with the news that everything
looked very bad. We decided to follow the trail opened by Coco and
to try to find another one which would lead to the Iquiri.

We have a mascot : Lolo, a little fawn. We will see if it survives.

APRIL 27

Coco's four hours turned out to be two and a half hours. We thought
we recognized one spot where there are many bitter orange trees as
the place marked on the map as Masico. Urbano and Benigno
continued opening up the trail and prepared a path for another
hour's march. It is intensely cold at night.

The Bolivian radio transmitted army reports which tell of the
death of a civilian guide, the dogs' trainer and the dog Rayo. They
give us two dead : one is assumed to be a Cuban nicknamed el
Rubio and the other a Bolivian. They confirm that Dantón is a
prisoner near Camiri; the others are almost sure to be alive with him.
h=950

86

We walked slowly until 15 : 00. By that time, the stream had dried out
and was taking another direction; so we halted. It was too late to
explore, so we went back towards the water to make camp. The
rest of our food will hardly last for four days. Tomorrow we will
try to get to the Nacahuasu along the Iquiri and we will have to
cut through the mountains.

Another probe was made along some ravines which we saw. The
result was negative. In this place, at least, we are in a canyon
without fissures. Coco thinks he saw a transversal canyon which he
did not explore; we will do so tomorrow with the troop.

After much delay, we decoded the whole of Message No. 35, which
contains a paragraph in which they ask me to authorize the putting
of my signature in an appeal supporting Vietnam and headed by
Bertrand Russell.

We started to attack the hill. The presumed canyon peters out in
some cliffs, but we located a crevice which we climbed. Night
surprised us near the top and we slept where we were, without being
too cold.

Lolo died, a victim of Urbano's impetuousness, who threw a rifle
at its head.

Radio Havana broadcasted news from some Chilean journalists
stating that the guerrillas are so strong that the cities are being
forced to take security measures and that two army trucks full
of food have been captured recently. *Siempre* magazine
interviewed Barrientos who, among other things, admitted that they
had some Yankee military advisers and that the guerrilla war had
emerged out of social conditions in Bolivia.

ANALYSIS OF THE MONTH
*The normal course of events took place, although we must regret
two great losses: el Rubio and Rolando. The death of the latter is a
severe blow, since I was thinking of delegating to him the command
of an eventual second front. We carried out four more actions; all of
them had positive results in general and one was very good: the
ambush where el Rubio died.*

On the other hand, our isolation continues to be total; various

*illnesses have undermined the health of some comrades, forcing us
to divide our forces, which has reduced our effectiveness a great
deal; we have not been able to contact Joaquín yet; our peasant
base is still undeveloped, although apparently a programme of
planned terror will succeed in neutralizing most of them, and their
support will come later. We have not had a single recruit and, apart
from the dead, we have lost el Loro, who disappeared after the
action at Taperillas.*

*Points noted in the military strategy which can be emphasized:
(a) Their controls have not been effective until now, and although
they make trouble for us, they still allow us to move around, due
to their own immobility and weakness; besides, after the last ambush
against the dogs and their trainer, they will presumably take much
more care before entering wooded areas; (b) the clamouring
continues, but now from both sides, and after the publication of my
article in Havana, nobody can have any doubt about my presence
here.*

*It seems certain that the North Americans will intervene here in
strength. They are already sending helicopters and, apparently, Green
Berets, although we haven't seen them here; (c) the army (at least
one or two companies in it) has improved its techniques; they
surprised us at Taperillas and were not demoralized at el Mesón;
(d) the mobilization of the peasants is non-existent, except in their
jobs as informers which bother us a little; but they are not very
rapid nor efficient; we can take care of them.*

*The status of el Chino has changed and he will be a combatant
until the formation of a second or a third front. Dantón and Carlos
fell victims of their own haste, almost desperation, to get out, and of
my lack of energy in trying to prevent them, so we have also cut our
communications with Cuba (Dantón) and we have lost our plan of
action in Argentina (Carlos).*

*To sum up: a month in which everything has evolved normally,
considering the standard development of a guerrilla war. The morale
of all the combatants is good because they have passed their first
test as guerrilla fighters.*

MAY, 1967

MAY 1

We celebrated May Day by opening up trails, but we progressed
very little; we haven't yet reached the point where the waters
divide.

88

In Havana, Almeida made a speech, praising me and the famous Bolivian guerrillas. It was a little too long, but good. We have enough food for three days. Nato killed a little bird with his sling today. We enter the era of the bird.

MAY 2

Day of slow progress and confusion about the geographical situation. Actually, we only travelled about two hours owing to the difficulty in making a path. From a height I was able to fix on a point near the Nacahuasu which indicates that we are well to the north, but there aren't any signs of the Iquiri. I gave orders to Miguel and Benigno to make a trail all day so as to try to reach the Iquiri or, at the least, the water, since we don't have any. We have five days' food left, but very little of it.

Radio Havana keeps up its information offensive against Bolivia, exaggerating the news.
h=reached 1,760 metres, we slept at 1,730.

MAY 3

During a day of continuously cutting through, which resulted in a usable path for a bit more than two hours, we arrived at a stream with quite a lot of water, which seems to flow to the north. Tomorrow, we will go on with cutting the trail simultaneously with exploring to see if the stream changes course. We have food left for only two days on short rations. We are at a height of 1,080 metres, 200 above the level of the Nacahuasu. We heard the distant sound of an engine from an unidentifiable direction.

MAY 4

During the morning, the trail was continued, while Coco and Aniceto explored the stream. They came back at about 13 : 00, confirming that the stream turned to the east and then to the south, so that it seemed to be the Iquiri. I ordered the machete men to be fetched and the waters to be followed downstream. We left at 13 : 30 and at 17 : 00 we halted, already sure that the general direction was east-north-east, so that it can't be the Iquiri unless it changes its course. The machete men reported that they had not come across any water, only more ridges; we decided to go forward with the impression that we are heading for the Grande river. We only shot a *cacaré*[1] which was divided up between the machete men, since it

---

[1] *Cacaré*: small bird of the forest, so named because it warns of the coming of men or animals with its cheeping.

was so small. Our food can only stretch for two days.

The radio gave the news of el Loro's capture; he was wounded in the leg, but his declarations are good up to now. Everything seems to indicate that he wasn't wounded in the house but somewhere else, presumably trying to escape.

h=980

We walked effectively for five hours, some twelve to fourteen kilometres, arriving at a camp made by Inti and Benigno. We are, then, in the Congrí creek which is not marked on the map, much more to the north than we thought. This raises several questions: where is the Iquiri? Could it be the one where Benigno and Aniceto were taken by surprise? Couldn't their attackers have been some of Joaquín's men? For the moment we are thinking of going to the Bear camp, where there should be two days' breakfast, and from there to the old camp. Today we killed two large birds and a *cacaré;* this means that we shall save our food and go on with a reserve for two days; soup powder in packets and tinned meat. Inti, Coco and the Doctor lay in a hide to hunt. News was broadcast that Debray will be tried by a military tribunal in Camiri as presumed head or organizer of the guerrilla; his mother is arriving tomorrow and there is a great fuss about the matter. Nothing about el Loro.

h=840

Our calculations about reaching the Bear camp proved faulty, since the distance from the stream to the little house was greater than anticipated and the trail was blocked, so we had to open it. We reached the little house at 16:30, after going over heights up to 1,400 metres with the men unwilling to march. We ate a very poor meal, the one before the last; we only shot a partridge which we gave to the machete man (Benigno) and to the two who followed him in the order of the march.

The news is centred on the Debray case.

h=1,100

We arrived early at the Bear camp and we found eight tins of milk there, which gave us a cheering breakfast. We took certain things out of the cave nearby, among them a Mauser for el Nato, who will

90

work our bazooka with its five anti-tank shells. He is unwell after a fit of vomiting. As soon as we got to the camp, Benigno, Urbano, León, Aniceto and Pablito went out to explore the little farm. We ate the last of the soup and meat, but we have a supply of lard that was in the cave. We saw some footprints and a little damage which indicates that soldiers have been here. The explorers came back at dawn with empty hands : the soldiers were in the little farm and had ruined the maize. (Six months have gone by since the official opening of the guerrilla with my arrival.)
h=880

Early in the morning I insisted that the caves should be repaired and the other tin of lard be brought down to fill bottles, because that is all we have to eat. At about 10 : 30, isolated shots were heard from the ambush. Two unarmed soldiers were coming up the Nacahuasu, and Pacho thought they were an advance party and fired, wounding one in the foot and the other slightly in the stomach. They were told that they had been shot at because they hadn't halted when told to do so; naturally, they hadn't heard a thing. The ambush was badly co-ordinated and Pacho's action wasn't very good; very nervous. I improved things by sending Antonio and some more men to the right side. The soldiers declared that they were located near the Nacahuasu, but in reality they were lying. At noon, two more were captured as they came running down by the Nacahuasu; they declared that they were running because they had gone out hunting and when they had returned by the Iquiri, they had found that their company had disappeared, so they had gone to look for it. They were also lying; in fact, they were camping in the hunting field and they were running off to look for some food at our farm because the helicopter had not come to supply them. We took loads of toasted and raw maize and four tins of fish, plus sugar and coffee from the first two prisoners. This solved our food problems for the day with the lard which we ate in great quantities; some men fell sick.

Later the sentry warned us of repeated reconnaissances by the soldiers, who went up to the river bend and returned. Everybody was tense when some 27 soldiers appeared. They had seen something out of the way and the group commanded by sub-lieutenant Laredo advanced; he himself started to fire and was killed on the spot along with two more recruits. Night was falling and our men advanced, capturing six soldiers; the rest withdrew.

91

The total figures are : three dead and ten prisoners, two of them
wounded; seven M-1s and four Mausers, personal equipment,
ammunition and a little food which served to stay our hunger along
with the lard. We slept where we were.

MAY 9

We woke up at 4 :00 (I didn't sleep) and freed the soldiers, after talking
to them. We took off their shoes, changed clothes with them and
sent off the liars in their underpants. They left for the little farm,
taking the wounded with them. At 6 :30 we completed our retreat
towards the monkeys' creek, taking the path by the cave, where we
left the spoils. We only have the lard left to eat. I felt faint and had
to sleep for two hours to be able to continue, slow and staggering.
The rest of us were in much the same way. We had lard soup at
the first watering place. The men are weak and many of them have
oedema. At night, the army gave its report of the action and named
its dead and wounded, but not its captured men. Large battles
were announced with heavy losses on our side.

MAY 10

We continued to advance slowly. When we got to the camp where we
buried el Rubio, we found tallow and the *charqui* we had left in bad
condition. We picked up everything; there weren't any signs of
soldiers. We crossed the Nacahuasu with precaution and started on
the road to Pirirenda by a ravine explored by Miguel, but by a
trail that is still incomplete. We stopped at 17:00 and ate the pieces
of *charqui* and the tallow.

MAY 11

The advance party left first; I stayed to listen to the news. A short
time later, Urbano came to report that Benigno had killed a wild
pig (a peccary); my permission was asked to light a fire and skin it;
we decided to stay and eat the animal, while Benigno, Urbano and
Miguel continued to make the trail towards the lagoon. At 14 :00 we
started marching again, making camp at 18 :00. Miguel and the
others went on ahead.

I must talk seriously with Benigno and Urbano, because the
first ate the contents of a tin the day of the fight and denied it, and
Urbano ate part of the *charqui* at el Rubio's camp.

The news announced that Colonel Rocha had been relieved; he
was in command of the 4th Division operating in the zone.
h = 1,050

92

We walked slowly. Urbano and Benigno opened up the track. At
15 : 00, we saw the lagoon about five kilometres away, and shortly
afterwards we found an old track. One hour later, we came to a huge
field of maize with pumpkins, but there was no water. We prepared
roasted and salted squash, and we husked the corn, then toasted it.
The scouts came with the news that they had fallen on Chicho's
house, the same one as the last time and mentioned as a good friend
in the diary of Lieutenant Henry Laredo. He wasn't at home, but
there were four peons and a maid, whose husband came to fetch her
and was detained by us. We cooked a large pig with rice and fritters
and pumpkins. Pombo, Arturo, Willy and Darío stayed guarding the
rucksacks. The bad thing was that we could not locate any water
outside the house.

   We withdrew at 5 : 30, moving slowly and with almost everybody
sick. The owner of the house had not arrived and a note was left
for him specifying his losses and expenses; for their work we paid
$10 to each of the peons and the maid.
h=950

Day of belching, farting, vomiting and diarrhoea; a real organ
concert. We stayed absolutely motionless, trying to digest the pig. We
have two tins of water. I was very ill until I vomited and felt better.
At night we ate maize fritters and roast pumpkin and the remnants
of yesterday's feast, that is, those of us who could eat. All the radio
bulletins insistently repeated the news that a Cuban landing in
Venezuela had been frustrated and that Leoni's government had
produced two of the captured invaders, giving their names and
ranks. I don't know them, but everything indicates that something
miscarried.

Early and unwillingly, we left for the Pirirenda lagoon along a path
found by Benigno and Camba while they were scouting. Before
setting off, I got everybody together and talked seriously to them
about the problems we had met, particularly about the food. I
criticized Benigno for having eaten a tin of food and denying it;
Urbano, for having eaten some *charqui* behind our backs; and
Aniceto for his insistence in joining in everything to do with food
and his reluctance to do anything else. During the course of the

93

meeting, we heard lorries approaching. In a cache nearby we stored some 50 squashes and 200 pounds of husked corn for our eventual needs.

While we were off the road, busy picking kidney beans, we heard the sound of shooting nearby and a little afterwards, we saw the air force ' bombing us ferociously,' but about two or three kilometres from our positions. We continued to climb a hillock and the lagoon came into sight, while the soldiers went on firing. At nightfall we approached a house, abandoned a little before by its occupants; it was well-stocked and had water. We ate a tasty chicken fricassee with rice, and we stayed there until 4 : 00.

MAY 15

Nothing to report today.

MAY 16

As soon as we started walking, I was hit by a terrible colic with vomiting and diarrhoea. They stopped it with Demarol and I lost consciousness while they carried me in a hammock. When I woke up, I felt much relieved, but I was runny all over like an unweaned baby. They lent me a pair of trousers, but as there was no water, I stank to high heaven. We spent all day there, while I drowsed. Coco and Nato went out exploring and found a road running south-north. At night we followed it while there was a moon and then we rested. We received Message No. 36, from which we inferred that our isolation is total.

MAY 17

We continued the march until 13 : 00, when we came to a saw-mill; there were traces that it had been abandoned about three days ago. It had sugar, maize, lard, cornmeal and water in barrels, seemingly transported from a long way away. We stayed in camp there, while the roads leaving the camp were explored; they end in the forest. Raúl has a sort of tumour on his knee which gives him too much pain to walk; he was given a strong antibiotic and tomorrow it will be lanced. We travelled some fifteen kilometres.
h=920

Roberto—Juan Martín   MAY 18
We spent the day in ambush, in case the workers or the army came; nothing happened. Miguel went out with Pablito and found water

about two hours from the camp down a side-road. We lanced Raúl's tumour, extracting 50 cc. of purulent fluid; we treated him generally against infection; practically, he cannot walk a step. I pulled out my first campaign tooth on this guerrilla campaign; the initial victim was Camba; it went well. We ate bread baked in a little oven and, in the evening, a barbarous stew which made me queasy again.

MAY 19

The advance party left early and took up positions in ambush on the crossroads. Afterwards, we left. One part replaced the advance party which returned to find Raúl and carry him to the crossroads; the other part of the centre went up to the watering place to leave the rucksacks and came back to fetch Raúl, who is making a slow recovery. Antonio explored a little down the stream and found a camp abandoned by the soldiers; there were some remnants of iron rations there. The Nacahuasu must not be far away, and I calculate that we must come out below the Congrí creek. It rained all night, surprising the experts.

We have food for ten days and there are pumpkins and maize in the vicinity.

h = 780

Camilo MAY 20

Day without movement. In the morning, the centre lay in ambush, and in the afternoon, the advance party, always under Pombo's command; he thinks that the position chosen by Miguel is a very bad one. Miguel explored downstream, finding the Nacahuasu two hours' march away without rucksacks. We heard a shot very clearly without knowing who fired it. On the banks of the Nacahuasu there were footprints from another army camp for a couple of platoons. There was an incident with Luis who protested that he was being punished by not getting an order to go to the ambush. Apparently, he reacted well.

At a press conference, Barrientos denied that Debray was a journalist and he announced that he will ask the Congress to re-establish the death penalty. Almost all the journalists and all the foreigners asked him about Debray; Barrientos defended himself with an incredible lack of astuteness. He is the most incompetent man one could imagine.

MAY 21

Sunday. No movement. We stayed in ambush, rotating ten men at midday. Raúl gets better slowly; we lanced him a second time, extracting 40 cc. of purulent fluid. He hasn't got a fever, but he is in pain and can hardly walk; that is my present worry. At night we ate luxuriously : stew, maize, flour, seasoned *charqui* and pumpkin sprinkled with meal.

MAY 22

As we had expected, Guzmán Robles, the man in charge of the saw-mill, appeared by noon, along with his chauffeur and a son in a battered jeep. At first it looked like the army sending scouts to see what was going on; but then he kept on giving way and he agreed to go to Gutiérrez at night, leaving his son as a hostage; he is to come back tomorrow. The advance party will remain in ambush all night and we will wait tomorrow until 15 :00. Then we will have to retreat, because the situation might become dangerous. We don't think the man is going to betray us, but we don't know if he will be clever enough to purchase things for us without raising suspicion. We paid him for all that we had taken from the factory. He gave us information about the situation in Tatarenda, Limón and Ipitá, where there are no soldiers except for one lieutenant in the last place. He hasn't been in Tatarenda, so he repeats what he has heard.

MAY 23

Day of tension. The man in charge of the saw-mill did not show up all day, and although there weren't any activities, we decided to retreat by night taking with us as a hostage a strapping lad of seventeen. We walked for about an hour along the track by moonlight and we slept on the road. We left with supplies of food for about ten days.

MAY 24

We got to the Nacahuasu, which was clear, in about two hours. We came out about four hours downstream at the Congrí creek. We walked slowly to fit in with Ricardo's slow and reluctant pace; today, Moro is lagging behind as well. We reached the same camp we had used on the first day of our first expedition. We didn't leave any footprints nor did we see any recent ones. The radio gave the news that Debray's petition for *habeas corpus* will be denied. According to my calculations, we are one or two hours from the Saladillo; when we get to the top, we will decide what to do.

96

MAY 25

We got to the Saladillo in one and a half hours without leaving any
traces. We walked about two hours upstream to the source of the
river. There we ate and went on at 15:30, walking for another two
hours until 18:00, when we camped at a height of 1,100 metres without getting to the top of the ridge. According to the boy, we still have
to go a couple of leagues to reach his grandfather's *chaco*[1] or, according to Benigno, we have a whole day of walking to Vargas's house on
the Grande river. Tomorrow we will decide.

MAY 26

After two hours' of walking and crossing the peak at 1,200 metres,
we got to the grandfather's *chaco*. Two labourers who were working
there had to be taken prisoner since they were walking towards us;
they turned out to be brothers-in-law of the old man, who was married
to a sister of theirs. Their ages : sixteen and twenty years old. They
gave us the information that the boy's father had bought the provisions, but that he had been arrested and confessed everything. There
are thirty soldiers patrolling in Ipitá. We ate a pig grilled with lard
and fried pumpkin, since there is no water in the area and it is transported in barrels from Ipitá. At night we left towards the *chaco*
owned by the two boys about eight kilometres away : four towards
Ipitá and four to the west. We got there by dawn.
h = 1,100.

MAY 27

Day of rest and a little desperation : of all the marvels they had
promised, they only had a little old sugar cane and the mill was
useless. As was to be expected, the old owner of the *chaco* arrived at
midday with his water cart for the pigs, saw something odd and
returned to the place where the rear party was in ambush, so they
took him prisoner with a labourer. They were our prisoners until
18:00, when we released them together with the younger of the
brothers. We ordered them to stay nearby until Monday and not to
say anything. We walked for two hours and slept in a cornfield,
having found the road which will take us to Caraguatarenda.

MAY 28

Sunday. We woke up early and started the march; in one and a half

---

[1] *Chaco* : a field cultivated with fruit trees or a peasant plot of land.

97

hours, we were at the limits of the *chacos* of Caraguatarenda, and we
sent Benigno and Coco to explore. A peasant saw them and they took
him prisoner. A short while later, we had a colony of prisoners who
were not very frightened. One old woman and her sons started
screaming until she was given orders to halt. Neither Pacho nor Pablo
had the courage to stop her, and she fled to the village. We took the
village at 14:00, placing ourselves at both ends of it. A short while
later a jeep from the oil company fell into our hands; in all we got
two jeeps and two trucks, half privately-owned and half belonging to
the oil company. We ate something and had some coffee, and after
fifty heated arguments, we left at 19:30 for Ipitacito. There we broke
into a shop and stole $500 worth of merchandise, leaving it in the
custody of two peasants after making out a very ceremonious promise
to pay. We continued on our wanderings, reaching Itay, where we
were very well-received at a house where we found the teacher who
owned the shop in Ipitacito, and we discussed prices. As I spoke with
them, it seemed to me that they recognized me; they had cheese and
some bread which they gave us with some coffee. But there was
something false about their welcome. We continued on to Espino
along the railway track to Santa Cruz, but the Ford truck had been
stripped of its front traction and broke down and it took us all
morning to get three leagues from Espino. The vehicle's engine blew up
completely two leagues from that place. The advance party took the
little shack and the jeep had to make four trips to get us all there.

MAY 29

The Espino settlement is relatively new, since the old one was obliter-
ated by a flood in '58. It is a Guaraní community, whose people are
very shy and speak or pretend to speak very little Spanish. There were
people from the oil company working nearby, and we got another
truck which could take all of us, but the opportunity was lost when
Ricardo got it stuck and it couldn't be pulled out. There was absolute
quiet as if we were in another world. Coco was given the duty of
finding out about the roads, but he brought us deficient and contradictory information, so that we were going to start a rather dangerous
journey, which would take us near the Grande river when, at the
last moment, things turned out not to be so and we must go to
Muchiri, a place where there is water. What with all the organizational
problems, we left at 3:30, the advance party in a jeep (six or seven
with Coco) and the rest on foot.

The radio gave the news of el Loro's escape from Camiri.

98

We arrived by day at the railway line, where we found out that the
road marked to take us to Muchiri did not exist. Looking about, at
500 metres from the crossing, we found a straight road for the oil
workers, and the advance party followed it in the jeep. As Antonio
was leaving, a young man with a shotgun and a dog appeared along
the railway line; when told to halt, he escaped. Faced with this news,
I left Antonio in ambush at the entrance to the road, and we stationed
ourselves 500 metres apart. At 11:45, Miguel arrived with the news
that he had walked twelve kilometres to the east without coming
across any houses or water, only a road that went to the north. I gave
him orders to explore it with three men in the jeep as far as ten
kilometres to the north and to come back before nightfall. At 15:00,
when I was quietly sleeping, I was woken up by some shots coming
from the ambush. Soon we got the news: the army had advanced
and had fallen into the trap. The result seems to be three dead and one
wounded. Antonio, Arturo, Nato, Luis, Willy and Raúl took part in it.
The latter was a bit weak. We retired on foot, walking the twelve
kilometres up to the crossing without finding Miguel. At that point,
we had the news that the jeep had broken down because of lack of
water. About three kilometres from there, we found it: we all urinated
into its tank and added a canteen of water, and so we were able to get
to our destination where Julio and Pablo were waiting. By 2:00,
everybody had met there around a fire in which we roasted three
turkeys and fried the pork. We kept one animal to test the water at
the water holes, just in case. We are coming down from a height of
750 metres; we are now at 650.

The jeep continued to work with our urine and the occasional water
canteen. Two things happened that changed our speed: the road
towards the north finished, so Miguel stopped the march; and one of
the security groups in a side road stopped the peasant Gregorio
Vargas, who was coming on his bicycle to do his job and set some
animal traps. The man's attitude wasn't all that clear, but he gave
valuable information about watering places. One of them was behind
us and I sent a group to fetch some water and food, with him as a
guide. While they were getting to the spot they sighted two army
trucks, which were quickly ambushed, apparently killing two men.
When el Nato shot the first blank bullet of his anti-tank grenade and
it missed fire, he put in a regular bullet and the whole thing exploded

under his nose, without harming him personally, but destroying the trombone. We continued our withdrawal without being harassed by the air force, and we walked about fifteen kilometres through the night, before finding the second watering place. The jeep gave its last gasp due to the lack of petrol and overheating. We spent the night eating. The army issued a *communiqué* admitting the death of a second lieutenant and a soldier yesterday and claiming they had ' seen ' some of us dead. I intend tomorrow to cross the railway and head for the mountains.
h=620

ANALYSIS OF THE MONTH
The negative point is the impossibility of establishing contact with Joaquín in spite of our wandering through the hills. There are signs that he has moved to the north.

From a military point of view, three new battles, with losses to the army and none to ourselves, as well as penetration into Pirirenda and Caraguatarenda, mean success. The dogs have proved incompetent and are withdrawn from circulation.

The most important characteristics are:

1. Total lack of contact with Manila, La Paz and Joaquín, which reduces us to the twenty-five men of the group.

2. Total failure to incorporate the peasants, although they are losing their fear of us, and we are winning their admiration. It is a slow and patient task.

3. Through Kolle, the party offers its collaboration, apparently without reservations.

4. The fuss about the Debray case has given more combat power to our movement than ten victorious fights.

5. The guerrilla goes on acquiring a powerful and sure morale which, well-managed, is a guarantee of success.

6. The army is still unorganized and its technique does not get substantially better.

News of the month: the imprisonment and escape of el Loro, who must now join us or go to La Paz to make contact.

The army issued the communiqué about the detention of all the peasants who collaborated with us in the Masicuri area. Now comes a stage where both sides will put pressure on the peasants, although in different ways; our success will produce a much-needed qualitative change in their development.

JUNE, 1967

I sent the men in the advance party to station themselves on the road and to scout for some three kilometres up to the crossing of the road to the oil fields. The air force has started circling round the area, confirming information on the radio that bad weather had made their operations difficult these last days and they would resume them now. They issued a curious report about two dead and three wounded; impossible to know whether they are old figures or new ones. After eating at 5 :00, we made for the railway. We covered seven or eight kilometres without trouble, walking one and a half hours along the railway line and then taking an abandoned path which should lead us to a *chaco* seven kilometres away; but everyone was very tired and we slept halfway there. During the march, we only heard one shot in the distance.
h=800

We covered the seven kilometres predicted by Gregorio and we got to the *chaco*. There we caught a sturdy pig and we killed it; but at that instant the cowherd of Braulio Robles, his son and two labourers appeared. One of them turned out to be a stepson of the owner, Symuní. We used their horses to carry the butchered pig for the three kilometres up to the stream, and there we detained them while we hid Gregorio, whose disappearance was known. When almost at the centre, we saw an army truck go by with two little soldiers and some barrels, an easy prey, but it was a day of pork and larking. We spent the night cooking and at 3:30 we released the four peasants, paying each $10 for their day. At 4:30, Gregorio left after waiting for food and more work and the $100 he received. The water in the stream is bitter.
h=800

We left at 6:30 by the left bank of the stream and marched until noon, when we sent Benigno and Ricardo to explore ahead to find a good place for an ambush. At 13:00, we took up our positions, Ricardo and myself each with a group in the centre, Pombo at the end and Miguel with all the advance party in an ideal place. At 14:30, a truck loaded with pigs passed, but we let it go by. At 16:20, a small truck with empty bottles, and at 17:00 an army lorry, the same one as

of the vehicle. I didn't have the heart to shoot them nor the presence of mind to stop the truck, so we let it go. At 18:00, we lifted the ambush and went on down the road until we reached the stream again. As soon as we arrived, four lorries passed in a row and then three more. Apparently without soldiers.

JUNE 4

We continued walking along the bank of the stream, with the intention of setting up another ambush if conditions were suitable; but we came to a track which took us to the west and we followed it; it went on through a dry river bed and it veered to the south. At 14:45, we stopped to make coffee and oatmeal by a small pool of muddy water, but it took a long time and so we decided to camp there. At night a strong south wind brought a steady drizzle which lasted all night.

JUNE 5

We left the track and we went on cutting through the woods under the persistent patter of the drizzle. We walked until 17:00, actually two and a quarter hours cutting dense undergrowth on the mountain slopes of this place. Fire became the almighty God of the day. We didn't eat anything the whole day; we kept the salty water in our flasks for tomorrow's breakfast.
h=250

JUNE 6

After a meagre breakfast, Miguel, Benigno and Pablito went to open up a way and to explore. At 14:00, Pablo came back with the news that he had found an abandoned *chaco* with cattle in it. We all started to march towards it and, by following the course of the stream, we crossed the *chaco* and came to the Grande river. From there we sent out scouts on a mission to take a house if they saw one nearby and if it was isolated. They did so, and the first report showed that we were three kilometres from Puerto Camacho, where there were about 50 soldiers. It can be reached by a path. We spent all night cooking pig and *locro;*[1] we didn't travel as much as we had hoped, and we were tired when we left, already in daylight.

JUNE 7

We walked at an easy pace, bypassing old pasture grounds, until

---

[1] *Locro*: soup made of rice, *charqui,* potatoes and other produce typical of the eastern region of Bolivia.

yesterday with two little soldiers wrapped up in blankets in the back the guide, one of the owner's sons, announced that there were no more. We continued along the beach until we found another *chaco,* which he hadn't mentioned, with squash, sugar cane, bananas and some kidney beans. There we camped. The boy who we are using as a guide started to complain about a severe stomach-ache; we don't know if it is genuine.
h=560

JUNE 8

We moved the camp about 300 metres, to stop having to keep a double watch on the beach and the *chaco* at the same time, although we learned later that the owner hadn't made a road there and he always came in a barge. Benigno, Pablo, Urbano and León went to try and make a path cutting across the cliff, but they came back in the afternoon with the news that it was impossible. I had to warn Urbano again about his griping. We decided to build a raft tomorrow, near the cliff.

News is being announced of the state of siege and of the threat by the miners, but all of it is meaningless.

JUNE 11

Day of absolute calm : we remained in ambush, but the army didn't advance; only a little plane flew over the area for a few minutes. It may mean that they are waiting for us at the Rosita. The trail across the ridge is now almost up to the top of the hill. Tomorrow we will go out anyway; we have enough food for five to six days.

JUNE 12

We believed in principle that we could reach the Rosita or at least the Grande river again, so we started the march. When we got to a small watering place, things became more difficult, so we stayed there, waiting for news. At 15:00 a report arrived that there was a larger watering place, but it was impossible to descend yet. We decided to stay here. The weather became worse and a strong south wind gave us a night of cold and rain. The radio gave us interesting news. The newspaper *Presencia* announced one dead and another wounded on the army's side in Saturday's clash. This is very good and almost certainly true, so we are keeping up our regular clashes with casualties. Another *communiqué* announced three more deaths, including Inti, one of the guerrilla chiefs, also the foreign composition of the guerrilla:

seventeen Cubans, fourteen Brazilians, four Argentines, three Peruvians. They have got the number of Cubans and Peruvians right. I must find out from where they obtained that information.
h=900

JUNE 13

We only walked for an hour, up to the next watering place, since the trail-openers didn't get either to the Rosita or to the river. It is very cold. Possibly they will get through tomorrow. We have just enough food for five days.

The interesting thing is the political convulsion in the country, the fabulous number of deals and counterdeals which are in the air. Seldom has the possibility of the guerrilla as a catalyst seemed as clear.
h=840

Celita (4?) JUNE 14

We spent the day in the cold watering place by the fire, waiting for news from Miguel and Urbano, who were opening the trail. The time set for moving was 15:00, but Urbano came back late to report that they had reached the stream and had seen some trail marks, which meant he thought he could get to the Grande river. We stayed in the same place eating our last stew; we only have left a ration of peanuts and three of stewed corn.

I am now 39 years old. The time is inexorably approaching in which I will have to reconsider my future as a guerrilla fighter; for the time being, I am ' all in one piece.'
h=840

JUNE 15

We walked for a little less than three hours to arrive at the banks of the Grande river; we recognised the spot which I reckon is about two hours from the Rosita; Nicolás, the peasant, said it was three kilometres. We gave him 150 pesos and the opportunity of going and he left like a rocket. We stayed in the same place where we had arrived; Aniceto went exploring and he thinks the river can be crossed. We ate peanut soup, and a little boiled palm heart cooked in lard; we have only enough stewed corn for three days.
h=610

JUNE 16

We had walked a kilometre when we saw the men of the advance party

104

on the opposite bank. Pacho had crossed by the ford which he found by exploring. We crossed with the icy water up to our waists and in something of a current, but without any incidents. An hour later we reached the Rosita, where there are some old footprints, apparently the army's. We found that the Rosita was deeper than we thought and there aren't any signs of the trail marked on the map. We walked for an hour in the icy water and we decided to camp, in order to eat the palm hearts and to try to locate a bee-hive that Miguel had found during a previous exploration; we didn't find the bee-hive, and we only ate stewed corn and *palmito* with lard. We still have food for tomorrow and the day after (stewed corn). We walked about three kilometres along the Rosita and another three along the Grande river. h=610

JUNE 17

We walked about fifteen kilometres along the Rosita in five and a half hours. On the way, we crossed four streams although only the Abapo-cito was marked on the map. We have found a lot of tracks of recent travellers. Ricardo killed a *hochi*[1], and with that and the stewed corn we had food for the day. There is still some stewed corn left for tomorrow, but presumably we will find a house.

JUNE 18

Many of us burnt our bridges, by eating all the stewed corn for break-fast. At eleven in the morning, after two and a half hours of walking, we came to a field of corn, *yuca*, sugar cane with a mill to grind it, squash and rice. We prepared a meal without proteins and we sent out Benigno and Pablito to explore. Two hours later Pablito came back with the news that they had found a peasant whose plot is about 500 metres from this one, and that behind him there were others coming who were taken prisoner when they reached us. By night we changed camp, sleeping in the boys' *chaco* situated at the beginning of the road which comes from Abapó, seven leagues from here. Their houses are on the fork of the Mosquera with the Oscura, on that last river ten to fifteen kilometres away.

JUNE 19

We walked at a slow pace for about twelve kilometres, to get to the hamlet formed by three houses and as many families. Two kilometres lower down, just at the fork of the Mosquera and the Oscura, lives a

---

[1] *Hochi* : a species of rodent originally from the Antilles.

family called Gálvez; the inhabitants have to be hunted down to be made to talk, as they are just like little animals. In general we were well received, but Calixto, named mayor by a military commission which passed through here a month ago, showed himself reserved and reluctant to sell various small items. By night, three pig dealers arrived carrying revolvers and Mauser rifles; they managed to get through the sentry from the advance party. Inti, who interrogated them, didn't take their weapons, and Antonio, who was guarding them, didn't do it with much care. Calixto assured us that he knows them and that they are tradesmen from Postrer Valle.

There is another river called the Suspiro which comes into the Rosita on its left bank; nobody lives along it.
h=680

JUNE 20

In the morning, Paulino, one of the boys from the *chaco* down below, informed us that the three men weren't dealers; there was one lieutenant and the other two didn't belong to the pig trade. He got this information through Calixto's daughter who is his fiancée. Inti went with several men and told them they had until 9 : 00 for the officer to come out; otherwise they would all be shot. The officer came out immediately, crying. He is a police lieutenant, sent with a rifleman and the teacher from Postrer Valle, who came voluntarily. They were sent by a colonel who is in that town with 60 men. Their mission was for a long journey of four days and included checking other points on the road to the Oscura. We thought of killing them, but I later decided to turn them back with a severe warning about the rules of war. On establishing how they could have got through, we found out that Aniceto had abandoned his post to call Julio and they got by in his absence; also Aniceto and Luis were found asleep while on guard. They were punished by serving on kitchen duty for seven days and going for one day without the roasted and fried pork and the stew, which is being served in large quantities. The prisoners will be stripped of all they have.

Mother   JUNE 21
After two days of continually pulling out teeth, during which I became notorious under the name of Fernando Tooth Extractor (alias) Chaco, I closed my dentist's surgery and we left in the afternoon, walking for a little more than an hour. For the first time in this war, I left riding a mule. The three prisoners were taken for an hour along the

106

track by the Mosquera and were stripped there of all their belongings including their watches and *abarcas*.[1] We thought of taking Calixto, the mayor, as a guide along with Paulino, but he was sick or pretended to be, and we left him with a severe warning which probably won't have much effect on him. Paulino has promised to get to Cochabamba with my message. He will be given a letter for Inti's wife, a coded message for Manila and the four *communiqués*. The fourth *communiqué* explains the composition of our guerrilla and clears up the lie about Inti's death. It is the [   ][2]. We will try to establish contact with the city. Paulino pretended to come as our prisoner. h=750

JUNE 22

We walked for three hours, making good progress, leaving the river Oscura or Morocos to reach a watering place named Pasiones. We checked on the map and everything indicated that we had at least six leagues to go to get to Florida or to the first place where there are houses, Piray. A brother-in-law of Paulino lives there, but he does not know the way. We thought we might go on, taking advantage of the moon; but it is not worthwhile due to the distance separating us. h=950

JUNE 23

We walked well for only an hour, since we lost the trail and it took us all morning and part of the afternoon to find it, and the rest of the day to open it up for tomorrow. St. John's Eve wasn't as cold as it's reputed to be.

Asthma is a serious threat to me, and we have a very small reserve of medicine. h=1,050

JUNE 24

We walked some twelve kilometres in all, four good hours. The track was good in parts and could be seen; in other parts, we had to invent it. We came down an incredible cliff, following the trail of some drovers who were herding cattle. We camped in a creek on the slopes of the Durán hill. The radio brings the news of fighting in the mines.

---

1 *Abarcas*: sandals worn by peasants and mule-drivers.
2 Blank in the original.

My asthma is getting worse.
h=1,200

JUNE 25

We continued along the track made by the drovers without catching up with them. By mid-morning, we found a burned pasture and an aeroplane flew over the area. We could not discover what connection there was between the two facts, but we went forwards and at 16:00 we arrived at el Piray, where Paulino's sister lives. There are three houses in this place; one was abandoned, one had nobody at home and in the third was the sister with her four children, but without her husband who had gone to Florida with Paniagua from the other house. Everything seemed normal. A daughter of Paniagua lived a kilometre away, and this was the house we chose for our camp, buying a calf and slaughtering it at once. Coco, with Julio, Camba and León, was sent to Florida to buy something, but they found that the army was there, some 50 men waiting to be reinforced up to 120 or 130 men. The owner of the house is an old man called Fenelón Coca.

The Argentinian radio gives news of 87 victims; the Bolivians are silent on the number of dead (in the Siglo XX Mine). My asthma is getting worse and now does not allow me to get any sleep.
h=780

JUNE 26

Black day for me. Everything seemed to be going quietly and I had sent five men to replace the ones in ambush on the road to Florida, when shots were heard. We rode there rapidly on the horses and found a strange sight : in the midst of a total silence, the bodies of four little soldiers were lying in the sun on the river sand. We couldn't take their weapons since we didn't know the enemy's position; it was 17:00 and we were waiting for nightfall to take them. Miguel sent a man to tell us that he had heard the sound of branches breaking on his left; Antonio and Pacho went there, but I gave orders that nobody was to shoot without being able to see. Almost at once, we heard firing which became general on both sides. I ordered the men to retreat, as we were bound to lose under these conditions. The retreat was delayed and news came that two of our men were wounded; Pombo in the leg and Tuma in the stomach. We took them quickly to the house to operate on them with what we had. Pombo's wound was superficial and only his lack of mobility will cause any headaches. Tuma had his liver destroyed as well as perforated intestines; he died during the operation. With him

108

I lost an inseparable comrade in all the preceding years; he was loyal
to the last, and I shall feel his absence from now onwards, almost as
if I had lost a son. When he fell, he asked them to give me his watch;
as they didn't do it because they were looking after him, he took it off
and gave it to Arturo. This gesture showed his wish to give it to the
son he has never seen, something I did with the watches of comrades
of mine who died before. I will wear it throughout the war. We put
the body on an animal and took it away to bury far from there.

We captured two new spies; a lieutenant of the carabiniers and one
of his men. They were given a warning and set free, only wearing their
underpants. This was due to a misunderstanding of my order to strip
them of anything which we could use. We left with nine horses.

JUNE 27

After we finished the painful task of giving Tuma a bad burial, we
followed the road, arriving at Tejería itself during the day. At 14:00
hours the advance party set out for a trip of fifteen kilometres, and we
left at 14:30. The trip was a long one for the last to leave, so that
night caught them and they had to wait for moonlight, reaching at
2:30 Paliza's house, from where the guides came.

We returned the animals to the owner of the house in Tejería; he is
a nephew of the old woman Paniagua, so he will send them back to
her.
h=850

JUNE 28

We found a guide who offered to take us to the crossroads leading
to Don Lucas's house for 40 pesos; but we stayed at a house on the
way, which had a watering place. We left late, but the last two,
Moro and Ricardo, took ages, and I couldn't listen to the news. We
kept up a rate of one kilometre an hour. According to the reports,
the army, or perhaps some radio station, talks of three dead and two
wounded in a clash with guerrilla fighters in the Mosquera area; it
must refer to our fight, but we could see, so clearly as to be nearly
certain, four corpses, unless one of them was pretending perfectly
to be dead.

We came to the house of a certain Zea; there was nobody at
home, but some cows were there with their calves penned in.
h=1,150

JUNE 29

I had a show-down with Moro and Ricardo for their delay,

especially with Ricardo. Coco and Darío left with their rucksacks on the horses. El Nato is in charge of all the animals, so he took his own rucksack, as well as mine and Pombo's on a mule. Pombo managed the journey relatively easily on a mare; we put him up in Don Lucas's house on top of the hill at 1,800 metres altitude; Lucas was there with his two daughters, one of whom suffers from goitre.

There are two other houses; one of them belongs to a part-time labourer who possesses almost nothing, while the other owner is well off. The night was rainy and cold. Barchelón is reported to be only half a day's march away, but the peasants who use the track say that it is in very bad condition. The owner of the house does not say the same thing and assures us that it can easily be put in order. The peasants came to see a man from another house and they were detained on suspicion.

On the road I talked with our troop, which now consists of 24 men. I cited el Chino as one of the first-class men, and I explained the significance of our losses and the personal loss that Tuma's death meant to me, since I almost considered him as a son. I criticized the lack of self-discipline and the slowness of the march and I promised to provide some more ideas so that our mistakes in the ambushes could not happen again : useless losses of life for being below standard.

JUNE 30

Old Lucas gave some information about his neighbours, from which we can deduce that the army has already been making its preparations out here. One of these, Andulfo Díaz, is the Secretary-General of the Peasants' Union of the area and is considered to be a supporter of Barrientos; another is an old chatterbox, whom we let go because he is paralysed, and another is a coward who may talk, according to his colleagues, to avoid complications. The old man promised to go with us and help us to open the way to Barchelón; the two peasants will follow us. We spent the day resting, since it was rainy and unpleasant.

On the political front, the most important thing is the official declaration of Ovando that I am here. He also said that the army was facing perfectly-trained guerrilla fighters, who included Vietcong commanders who had defeated the best North American regiments. He based his statements on Debray's, who apparently has spoken more than is necessary, although we cannot know the implications of this, nor the circumstances in which he said what he

110

has said. There are rumours that el Loro has been assassinated. They attribute to me the inspiration for the planned miners' revolt, to be co-ordinated with the Nacahuasu action. Things are getting better; within a short while I will cease to be ' Fernando Tooth Extractor.'

We received a message from Cuba explaining the slow development of the guerrilla organization in Peru, where they hardly have any weapons or men, although they have spent a lot of money and speak of a supposed guerrilla network between Paz Estensoro, a Colonel Seoane and a certain Rubén Julio, a rich man in the movement from the Pando area. They would be in Guayaramerin. It is the [   ].[1]

ANALYSIS OF THE MONTH
The negative points are: the impossibility of making contact with Joaquín and the gradual loss of men, each one of whom constitutes a serious defeat, although the army doesn't realize it. We fought two small skirmishes in the month, causing the army to lose four dead and three wounded, if we can go by their reports.

The most important characteristics are:

(1) The almost total lack of contacts continues, which reduces us now to the 24 men who make up our group, with Pombo wounded and our mobility reduced.

(2) We continue to feel the lack of peasant recruits. It is a vicious circle: to get this recruitment we need to be permanently in action in a populated area and for that we need more men.

(3) The legend of the guerrilla grows like wildfire; already we are invincible supermen.

(4) The lack of contact extends to the Party, although we have made an attempt through Paulino that may bring some results.

(5) Debray continues in the news, but more in relation to my case, that now I appear as the leader of this movement. We will see the result of this step of the government's and whether it is positive or negative for us.

(6) The morale of the guerrilla stays firm and the will to fight increases. All the Cubans set an example in combat and there are only two or three feeble Bolivians.

(7) The army continues to be nothing militarily speaking, but we must not underestimate how it is working on the peasants, since it

---

[1] Illegible in the original.

111

transforms all the members of a community into informers, either by fear or by lying to them about our objectives.

(8) The massacre in the mines clears up much of the view for us and, if it can be proclaimed widely, it will be a great factor in enlightening people.

Our most urgent task is to re-establish contact with La Paz, to restock our medical and military supplies and to recruit about 50 to 100 men from the city, even if the number of combatants is never more than ten or fifteen people in action.

JULY, 1967

JULY 1

Before the day had completely cleared, we set out for Barchelón, called Barcelona on the map. Old Lucas helped us a bit in repairing the road but, in spite of everything, it remained pretty steep and slippery. The advance party left in the morning and we set off at noon, spending all the afternoon in going up and down the ravine. We had to stop and sleep in the first *chaco*, separated from the advance party who went on ahead. There were three little boys called Yépez, very shy.

At a press conference, Barrientos admitted I was here, but forecast that I would be liquidated in a few days' time. He spoke his usual string of idiocies, calling us rats and vipers and repeating his intention of punishing Debray.

We detained a peasant called Andrés Coca, whom we met on the way and took with us along with the other two, Roque and his son Pedro.

h = 1,550

JULY 2

We joined the advance party in the morning; it had camped on the hill in the house of Don Nicomedes Arteaga, where there is an orange grove and where they sold us cigars. The main house is down below on the Piojera river, and there we went after a huge meal. The Piojera river is completely enclosed in a canyon and it can only be followed on foot down towards the Angostura; the way out is towards la Junta, another point on the same river, where it cuts through a rather high hill. It is an important point since it is a cross-roads. This place is at an altitude of only 950 metres and is much more temperate; here small ticks give way to small mosquitos. The settlement consists of Arteaga's house and his sons' houses; they

112

have a small coffee plantation where local people come to work for
a share of the crop. There are now about six labourers from the San
Juan area.

Pombo's leg is not healing as fast as it should, probably owing
to the endless trips on horseback, but he hasn't had any complications
and we need not fear any now.

JULY 3

We stayed on there all day, trying to give Pombo's leg a good rest.
As we pay high prices for what we buy, the peasants yield to
self-interest in spite of their fear and find the things for us. I took
some photographs, which was fascinating to everybody; we will
have to see how to develop, print and get the copies back to them :
three problems. An aeroplane flew over in the morning and at night
somebody spoke of the danger of night bombing raids and everybody
went off in the dark; but we stopped them and explained that there
wasn't any danger. My asthma keeps up its fight against me.

JULY 6

We left early towards Peña Colorada, crossing an inhabited area
in which the people were terrorized to see us. By nightfall, we arrived at
the Alto de Palermo, 1,600 metres high, and we started to climb
down to the point where there is a little grocery; we bought things
there just in case. As it was night, we came out on the main road
where there is only a tiny house belonging to an old widow. The
advance party botched the taking of the house due to indecision.
The plan was to take a vehicle coming from Sumaipata, find out
what was going on there, proceed there with the driver of the
vehicle, take the DIC, make some purchases at the chemist, raid
the hospital, buy some tins and sweets, and then return.

We changed our plan because no vehicles were coming from
Sumaipata, and we got the news that vehicles were not being
halted in that district, which meant that the controls had been
lifted. Ricardo, Coco, Pacho, Aniceto, Julio and el Chino were
chosen for the action. Without any trouble, they stopped a lorry that
was coming from Santa Cruz, but another one which was passing
stopped to offer help and had to be detained as well. An argument
then started with a lady who was travelling on the lorry with her
daughter and did not want to make her get out. A third lorry stopped
to see what was going on and as the road was obstructed by now, a
fourth lorry stopped because of the general indecision. Things were

113

settled and the four lorries parked on one side of the road and a driver said that it was a rest for him, when he was asked. The men went in one of the lorries to Sumaipata, where they captured two soldiers and the chief of the post, Lieutenant Vacaflor. The sergeant was forced to give the password and a lightning action captured the post with its ten soldiers after a brief exchange of fire with a soldier who resisted. They succeeded in taking five Mausers and one 1 Z-B-30 and drove away with the ten prisoners, leaving them naked one kilometre from Sumaipata. From the supply angle, the action was a failure; el Chino let himself be influenced by Pacho and Julio, and nothing useful was bought. As for the medicines, they didn't get any of the things I need, although they did get the most indispensable ones for the guerrilla. The action took place in front of the whole town and a group of travellers, so the news will spread like wildfire. At two in the morning we were on our way back with the booty.

JULY 7

We marched without resting until we reached a sugar-cane field where a man had received us well the last time we were there, a league from Ramón's house. Fear is still running through the people; the man sold us a pig and was pleasant, but he warned us that there were 200 men in Los Ajos and that his brother had just come from San Juan and announced that there were 100 soldiers there. I wanted to extract some of his teeth, but he preferred not to have it done. My asthma is getting worse.

JULY 8

We took precautions, as we travelled from the house in the sugar cane to the Piojera river, but everything was clear and there weren't any signs of soldiers; the people coming from San Juan denied that there were any soldiers there. Apparently the man had played a trick on us to make us leave. We walked about two leagues along the river to el Piray and on from there another league to the cave, where we arrived when night was falling. We are near el Filo.

I gave myself injections from time to time so that I could continue; in the end I used a solution of adrenalin at 1 : 900 prepared for collyrium. If Paulino hasn't carried out his mission, we will have to go back to the Nacahuasu to look for medicines for my asthma.

The army gave out its report on the action, admitting to one man dead, which must have happened in the shooting when Ricardo, Coco and Pacho took the little military post.

When we left, we lost our way and spent the morning looking for it.
At midday we followed a rather obscure trail which took us to the
greatest height yet reached, 1,840 metres; shortly afterwards, we
arrived at an old hut where we spent the night. There is no
certainty about the road to el Filo. The radio gave the news of a
fourteen point accord between the workers of the Catavi and Siglo
XX and the Empresa Comibol mines; this means a total defeat for
the workers.

We left late, because we had lost a horse, which turned up later.
We took a rarely-used path which reached a maximum height of
1,900 metres. At 15 : 30 we reached an old hut where we decided
to spend the night, but we got a disagreeable surprise when we
found that the trails were ending. Some unused trails were explored,
but they did not lead anywhere. In front of us, there are some
chacos, which could be el Filo.

The radio gives the news of a clash with guerrillas in the area of
el Dorado, which is not marked on the map and is located somewhere between Sumaipata and the Grande river. They admit to one
wounded and give us two dead.

The declarations of Debray and el Pelado, however, are not good;
worst of all, they have admitted the intercontinental aims of the
guerrilla, something which they should not have done.

Coming back on a day of fog and rain, we lost all the tracks and
became absolutely separated from the advance party which got
down by opening an old trail. We killed a calf.

We spent all day waiting for news from Miguel, but Julio only
arrived at nightfall with the news that they had climbed down to
a stream that ran to the south. We stayed in the same place. My
asthma kept on giving me trouble.

The radio now broadcasts more news which seems true in its
most important bit; it speaks of a combat on the Iquiri, with one
man dead on our side whose body has been taken to Lagunillas.
Their delight over the corpse indicates that there is some truth in
the story.

In the morning, we descended a steep hill, made slippery by the bad weather. We met up with Miguel at 11 : 30. I had sent Camba and Pacho to explore a trail which diverged from the one running along the course of the stream and they returned an hour later with the news that they had seen fields and houses and that they had gone into an abandoned house. We transferred there and followed the course of the little stream until we came to the first house, where we spent the night. The owner of the house arrived later and informed us that a woman, the mother of the local magistrate, had seen us and must have already reported us to the soldiers who were at the settlement of el Filo itself, a league away from here. We kept watch all night.

It drizzled all night and all day, but we left at noon taking two guides with us, Pablo, the mayor's brother-in-law, and Aurelio Mancilla, the man from the first house. The women were left behind, weeping. We came to a point where the roads fork; one went to Florida and Moroco, the other to Pampa. The guides suggested that we take the one to Pampa, from which we could take a recently opened trail to the Mosquera. We accepted their choice, but when we had walked about 500 metres, a little soldier and a peasant with a load of flour on a horse appeared. They had a message to the 2nd lieutenant in el Filo from his colleague in Pampa where there are 30 soldiers. We decided to change our course and we took the road to Florida, making camp a short while later.

The PRA and the PSB are withdrawing from the revolutionary front and the peasants are warning Barrientos about an alliance with the Falange. The government is rapidly disintegrating. It's a pity we do not have 100 men more at this moment.

We walked very little due to the bad condition of the road, abandoned for many years. On Aurelio's advice, we killed one of the magistrate's cows and had a splendid meal. My asthma has let up a little.

Barrientos announced Operation Cintia, which is supposed to liquidate us within a few hours.

We started marching very slowly, due to the intensive work of
cutting our way through, and the animals suffered a lot because of
the bad road, but we arrived without any major incidents. We
ended our journey in a canyon where it is impossible to get through
with horses carrying loads. Miguel and four men from the advance
party went on ahead and slept further on.

There was no news worth mentioning on the radio. We crossed
a height of 1,600 metres near the Durán hill which we kept on our
left.

We continued to progress slowly, for we lost our way. We had
hoped to arrive at an orange grove pointed out to us by the guide,
but when we got there, we found that the trees were shrivelled.
There was a puddle which allowed us to camp. We did not cover
more than three hours of march effectively. My asthma is much
better. Apparently we will meet up with the road we used to get to
el Piray. We are on the side of the Durán.
h=1,560

After an hour of marching, the guide lost the route and declared
that he didn't know any further. At last we found an old path and,
while it was being opened, Miguel cut his way through the forest
and followed it through to its meeting with the Piray road. When
we arrived at a little stream where we camped, we released the three
peasants and the little soldier, after giving them a lecture. Coco went
off with Pablito and Pacho to see whether Paulino had left anything
in the hole; they should be back by tomorrow night if everything
works according to plan. The little soldier says he is going to desert.
h=1,300

We completed the short stage to the old camp and we stayed there.
We reinforced the sentries and waited for Coco, who arrived after
18 : 00 hours announcing that nothing had changed; the rifle was
in place and there were no traces of Paulino. There were, however,
signs that troops had passed by; they had also left tracks on the part
of the road we are on.

The news is about a tremendous political crisis and I don't see

117

where it is going to end. Meanwhile, the agricultural syndicates of
Cochabamba have formed a political party ' of Christian
inspiration ' which supports Barrientos who is asking, almost
imploring, to be ' allowed to govern for four years.' Siles Salinas is
threatening the opposition by saying that our coming to power will
cost everyone's head, by calling for national unity, and by declaring
the country in a state of war. He seems to be on the one hand
imploring and on the other a demagogue; perhaps he is preparing
a coup.

JULY 20

We moved very cautiously until we reached the first two little
houses where we found one of Paniagua's boys and Paulino's son-in-
law. They didn't know what Paulino was up to, except that the army
was looking for him for having been our guide. The footprints
indicate that a group of 100 men passed by, a week after we had
gone on towards Florida. Apparently the army suffered three dead
and two wounded in the ambush. Coco, Camba, León and Julio
were sent to scout in Florida and to buy what they could find there.
Coco came back at 4:00 with some food and a certain Melgar, the
owner of two of our horses; he offered to be of service to us and
gave us detailed and reliable information containing the following
facts: four days after our departure, Tuma's body was discovered,
eaten by the animals; the army advanced only the day after the
fight, after the naked lieutenant had shown up; the action in
Sumaipata is known down to the last detail with trimmings and is
a cause of mockery by the peasants; they found Tuma's pipe as well
as some of his belongings lying around; a major named Soperna
seemed to half-sympathize with us or admire us; the army reached
Coco's house, where Tuma had died, and from there went on to
Tejería, before returning to Florida. Coco thought of using the
man to deliver a letter, but I thought it more prudent to test him
first by sending him to buy some medicines. This man, Melgar, told
us about a group which is coming towards here, including a woman;
he had learned this from a letter sent by the magistrate of Río
Grande to the one here. As this man was on his way to Florida, we
sent Inti, Coco and Julio to interview him. He denied that he had
news of another group, but he generally confirmed the evidence of
Melgar. We spent a dreadful night because of the rain. The radio
gave the news that the body of the dead guerrilla fighter had been
identified as Moisés Guevara, but Ovando was very cautious about

118

this at a press conference and said that the Ministry of the Interior was responsible for the identification. There is a possibility that the whole thing may be a farce and the supposed identification an invention.
h=680

JULY 21

We spent the day quietly. We talked with the old man Coco about the cow which he had sold us when it did not belong to him, and then he said that he had not been paid. He emphatically denied the fact; but we forced him to pay.

We went to Tejería by night and bought a big pig and cakes of molasses. The people gave a good reception to Inti, Benigno and Aniceto, the ones who went there.

JULY 22

We left early, with shoulders and animals overloaded, and with the intention of misleading everybody about whether we were really here. We left the road that goes to Moroco and took the one to the lagoon, one or two kilometres to the south. Unfortunately, we didn't know the rest of the way and we had to send out scouts. Meanwhile, Mancilla and the boy Paniagua appeared by the lagoon, herding cattle. They were forbidden to say anything, but things are very different now. We walked for a couple of hours, sleeping beside a stream, which has a path to the south-east along its course and other worse ones going southwards.

The radio announces that the wife of Bustos (Pelao) confirms that he saw me here, but she says that he came with other intentions.
h=640

JULY 23

We stayed in the same camp while two possible ways were ordered explored. One of them led to the Seco river, at a point where the waters of el Piray join it and the sand has not absorbed them all yet, that is to say, between the ambush which we set and Florida. The other trail leads to a hut about two or three hours' march from here and, according to Miguel who did the scouting, it is possible to come out at the Rosita from there. We shall take that road tomorrow, which may be one of Melgar's, according to the stories he told to Coco and Julio.

119

We travelled about three hours following the trail already explored, which made us scale heights of 1,000 metres; we camped at a height of 940 metres on the bank of a stream. Here the roads end and we will have to spend the whole of tomorrow looking for the best way out. There are a series of *chacos* here under cultivation which show a certain similarity with those of Florida; this could be the place called Canalones. We are trying to decode a long message from Manila. Raúl spoke at the graduation of officers at the Máximo Gómez School and, among other things, refuted the qualifications of the Czechs about my article on the Vietnams. My friends are calling me a new Bakunin, and deploring the blood spilled and that which will be spilled in the case of three or four Vietnams.

JULY 25

We spent the day resting, sending three two-men groups to explore various points. Coco, Benigno, and Miguel were in charge of doing it. Coco and Benigno came out at the same place and from there the road to Moroco can be taken. Miguel informed us that the stream absolutely certainly flows into the Rosita, and that we can travel along it, although only by cutting our way through with machetes.

Two actions are reported, one in Taperas and the other in San Juan del Potrero; these could not have been carried out by the same group, and the question is raised whether they really exist and whether the facts are true.

JULY 26

Benigno, Camba and Urbano were commissioned to make a trail along the stream, avoiding Moroco; the rest of the men stayed in the camp and the centre set up an ambush behind. No incidents.

The news of the action at San Juan del Potrero was broadcast on foreign stations with full details : fifteen soldiers and a colonel were captured, looted and set free — our technique. The place is on the other side of the Cochabamba-Santa Cruz highway. At night I gave a little talk about the significance of the 26th of July; a rebellion against the oligarchies and against revolutionary dogmas. Fidel briefly mentioned Bolivia.

JULY 27

We were completely ready to go and the men in the ambush had been given the order to leave it automatically at 11 :00, when Willy

120

came a few minutes before that hour, announcing that the army was there. Willy himself, Ricardo, Inti, el Chino, León and Eustaquio, went there and joined Antonio, Arturo and Chapaco to carry out the action. It worked in this way : eight soldiers appeared at the top, walked towards the south following a small old path and returned, firing some mortar shells and making signals with a rag. At one moment, shouting for a certain ' Melgar ' was heard, who could well be the one from Florida. After resting for a while, the eight little soldiers started marching towards the ambush. Only four of them fell into it, since the rest were slightly lagging behind; three were certainly killed and the fourth probably, wounded anyway. We pulled back without taking their weapons or equipment because of the difficulty of picking them up, and we went downstream. When we came to a fork with another little canyon, we set up a new ambush; the horses were sent on to where the trail ended.

My asthma gave me a bad time and the miserable sedatives are going to run out.
h=800

JULY 28

Coco, Pacho, Raúl and Aniceto were sent to cover the outlet of the river which we think is the Suspiro. We travelled a little, opening up a trail through the fairly narrow canyon. We camped separated from the advance party, since Miguel advanced too much for us to be able to follow with the horses, which sank in the sand or suffered from the stones.
h=760

JULY 29

We went on walking through a canyon which sloped down towards the south with good hiding places on its sides and in an area with enough water. At approximately 16 :00 we met Pablito who informed us that we were at the outlet of the Suspiro, but there was nothing to report. For a moment, I thought that this canyon wasn't that of the Suspiro because it ran mainly in a southerly direction, but it turned west at its last bend and ran into the Rosita.

At about 16 :30 the rear party arrived and I decided to continue the journey by moving away from the outlet, but I didn't dare to ask the men for the effort necessary to get beyond Paulino's *chaco,* so we made camp on the sides of the road, one hour's march from the Suspiro's outlet. At night, I passed the word to el Chino to refer to his country's Independence on the 28th of July, and then I explained why the camp was badly situated, giving the order to rise at 5 :00 and go to take Paulino's *chaco*.

Radio Havana spoke of an ambush in which some members of the army fell; these were removed by helicopter, but I couldn't hear the news well.

JULY 30

My asthma disturbed me a lot and I lay awake the whole night. At 4 :30, when Moro was making some coffee, he warned us that he had seen a light moving across the river. Miguel, who was awake to change sentries, and Moro went off to detain the travellers. From the cooking place, I heard the following exchange : Hey, who goes there?

— The Trinidad detachment.

The firing started instantly. A moment later, Miguel brought in an M-1 and a cartridge belt from a wounded man and the news that there were 21 men on the way to Abapó and 150 men in Moroco. We caused them further losses, but we could not count these in the general confusion. It took a long time to load the horses and el Negro got lost with a hatchet and a mortar which had been taken from the enemy. It was already about 6 :00 in the morning and we were losing more and more time, because some of the loads were slipping off. The final result was that the last crossings were made under fire from the little soldiers, who had got their nerve back. Paulino's sister was in her *chaco* and received us very calmly, telling us that all the men in Moroco had been arrested and were in La Paz.

I hurried up the men and crossed the river canyon with Pombo, again under fire, because we could organize resistance where the trail ended. I sent Miguel with Coco and Julio to take up a forward position, while I spurred on the cavalry. Seven men from the advance party, four from the rear party, and Ricardo were left behind to cover our retreat and to reinforce the defence. Benigno, with Darío, Pablo and Camba, was on the right flank; the rest were coming by the left. I had just ordered a halt to rest in the first available position, when Camba came with the news that Ricardo and Aniceto had fallen crossing the river. I sent Urbano, el Nato and León with two horses to look for Miguel and Julio, leaving Coco as a sentry in front. These got through without getting my instructions and, after a while, Camba came back again with the news that they had been taken by surprise together with Miguel and Julio, that

122

the soldiers had advanced a great deal, and that they had retreated
and were waiting for my orders. I sent them Camba again and
Eustaquio as well; only Inti, Pombo, el Chino and myself stayed on.
At 13 : 00 I sent for Miguel leaving Julio as the advance sentry, and
I retired with the group of men and horses. As I was climbing up to
Coco's post, the news reached us that all the survivors had shown up:
Raúl was dead, and Ricardo and Pacho wounded. This was what
had happened : Ricardo and Aniceto were rashly crossing the
clearing, when the first of them was wounded. Antonio organized a
line of fire and Arturo, Aniceto and Pacho managed to rescue
Ricardo, but Pacho was wounded and Raúl killed by a bullet through
the mouth. The retreat was difficult, what with dragging along the
two wounded and with little help from Willy and Chapaco,
especially from the last. Then they rejoined Urbano and his group
with the horses and Benigno with his men, leaving the other flank
unguarded through which the soldiers advanced to surprise Miguel.
After a painful march through the forest, they came to the river
and united with us. Pacho came on horseback, but Ricardo could
not mount and had to be carried in a hammock. I sent Miguel with
Pablito, Darío, Coco and Aniceto to hold the outlet of the first
stream on the right bank, while we looked after the wounded. Pacho
had a superficial wound which penetrated his buttocks and the skin
of his testicles, but Ricardo was seriously wounded and our last
plasma had been lost with Willy's rucksack. At 22 :00 Ricardo died
and we buried him near the river in a well-hidden place so that the
soldiers would not find him.

JULY 31

At 4:00 we left along the river and crossed by a short cut
and went on downriver without leaving any tracks. We arrived
in the morning at the stream where Miguel was ambushed; he had
not heard the order and had left footprints. We travelled some four
kilometres upriver and we went into the forest, erasing our tracks
and camping near a tributary of the stream. At night I explained
our mistakes in the action : (1) the bad location of the camp; (2)
our waste of time, which allowed them to shoot at us; (3) our excess
of confidence which made Ricardo and then Raúl fall in the rescue;
(4) our lack of determination in saving the equipment. We lost eleven
rucksacks containing medical supplies, field-glasses and some general
equipment such as the tape-recorder for copying the messages from
Manila, Debray's book annotated by me and a book by Trotsky, not

123

counting the political value of this to the government and the
confidence it will give to the soldiers. We calculate about two dead
and up to five wounded on their side, but there are two contradictory
pieces of news : one from the army, admitting to four dead and
four wounded on the 28th, and the other from Chile, speaking of
six wounded and three dead on the 30th. The army later issued
another report announcing the capture of a corpse and the recovery
of a sub-lieutenant from the danger list. Of our dead, Raúl hardly
counts, considering his introspective nature; he wasn't a good fighter
or worker, but he was always interested in political problems, even
if he never asked any questions. Ricardo was the most undisciplined
of the Cuban group and the one who showed the least decision when
facing up to everyday sacrifices, but he was an excellent fighter and
an old comrade in adventure at the first failure at Segundo, in the
Congo and now here. His quality makes him another important loss.
We are 22, with two wounded, Pacho and Pombo, and myself with
my asthma at full steam ahead.

ANALYSIS OF THE MONTH
*The same negative points as last month continue. These are: the
impossibility of contacting Joaquín and the exterior world and the
loss of men. We are now 22, with three disabled including myself,
which lessens our mobility. We have had three clashes, including the
taking of Sumaipata, inflicting on the army losses of some seven dead
and ten wounded; these are approximate figures taken from confused
reports. We have lost two men with one wounded.*

The most important characteristics are:

(1) Total lack of contact continues.

*(2) We continue to feel the lack of peasants joining us, although
there are some encouraging symptoms in the reception we got from
the peasants we already know.*

*(3) The legend of the guerrillas is acquiring continental
dimensions; Onganía has closed the Argentinian frontiers and Peru
is taking precautions.*

(4) The attempt to establish contact through Paulino failed.

*(5) The morale and combat experience of the guerrilla increases
with each fight: Camba and Chapaco remain feeble.*

*(6) The army continues to put its foot in it, but there are units
which seem to be more aggressive.*

*(7) The political crisis in the government grows, but the U.S.A.
is handing out small credits which are a great help by Bolivian*

124

standards and serve to ease the discontent.
The most urgent tasks are: Re-establish contacts, recruit
combatants and get medicines.

AUGUST, 1967

Quiet day : Miguel and Camba started on the path, but they
progressed only a little over a kilometre due to the difficult terrain
and the vegetation. We killed a tricky colt which ought to give us
meat for five to six days. We dug some small trenches to set an
ambush for the army if they came that way. The idea is to let
them pass if they come tomorrow or the day after, and if they don't
discover the camp; then we'll attack them afterwards.
h=650

The path seems to have progressed well thanks to Benigno and
Pablo who are going on with it. They took almost two hours to come
back to camp from the far end of the path. There is no news of us
on the radio, since they announced the transfer of the corpse of an
' anti-social ' person. My asthma is very hard on me and I have used
the last anti-asthmatic injection; I only have tablets left for about
ten days.

The work on the path turned out a fiasco; Miguel and Urbano only
took 57 minutes to get back today; they progressed very slowly.
There is no news. Pacho is recovering well but I, on the other hand,
am worse. I found the day and the night very painful and I cannot
see any quick cure for me. I tried an intravenous injection of
novacaine without any result.

The men reached a canyon which runs towards the south-east and
may come out on the streams that flow to the Grande river. From
tomorrow onward two pairs will go out cutting and Miguel will
climb our canyon to explore what seem to be old *chacos*. My asthma
has somewhat improved.

Benigno, Camba, Urbano and León split up into two couples to make
more progress, but they came to a stream which flows into the Rosita

125

and they had to go on cross country. Miguel went to explore the *chaco,* but could not find it. We finished the horse meat; we will try to fish tomorrow and the day after tomorrow we will sacrifice another horse. Tomorrow, we will advance towards the new watering place. My asthma never lets up. In spite of my reluctance to separate ourselves, I will have to send a group ahead. Benigno and Julio offered themselves as volunteers; el Nato's position must be examined.

AUGUST 6
We made the transfer to the other camp; unfortunately, there were not three hours of trail, but only one, which means that we are still far away. Benigno, Urbano, Camba and León went on using their machetes, while Miguel and Aniceto went off to explore the new stream as far as its fork with the Rosita. They had not returned by night, so we took precautions, especially as I had heard something like a mortar shot far away. Inti, Chapaco and then myself said some words referring to today's date, that of Bolivian Independence. h=720

AUGUST 7
By 11:00 I had given up Miguel and Aniceto for lost, and I ordered Benigno to advance very cautiously towards the outlet on the Rosita and to investigate a little the direction they had taken, if they had reached there at all. At 13:00, however, the lost men appeared; they had simply run into difficulties on the road and night had come on them before reaching the Rosita. Miguel gave me a bitter pill to swallow. We stayed on the same site, but the trail-openers found another stream and we will transfer there tomorrow. The old horse Anselmo died today, and now we only have one left to carry our stuff. My asthma continues without varying, but the medecines are being used up. I will take a decision tomorrow about sending a group to the Nacahuasu.

Today completes nine months exactly since the guerrilla was formed with our arrival. Of the six first ones in it, two are dead, one has disappeared and two are wounded, I with an asthma which I don't know how to stop.

AUGUST 8
We walked for about an hour effectively, which seemed more like two to me because of the weariness of the little mare; at one stage, I drove my little knife into her neck, opening quite a wound. The new

126

camp must be the last with water before getting to the Rosita or the Grande river; the machete men are about 40 minutes from here (two to three kilometres). I picked a group of eight men to carry out the following mission : they are to leave here tomorrow and travel the whole day; on the following day, Camba will return with news of what there is; on the next day, Pablito and Darío are to come back with news of that day. The other five will keep on as far as Vargas's house, and Coco and Aniceto will return from there to say how things are going; Benigno, Julio and el Nato will go on to the Nacahuasu to look for my medecines. They must be very careful to avoid ambushes; we will be following them. A rendezvous will be set up at Vargas's house or a bit further up, depending on our speed, and at the stream that faces the cave by the Grande river, the Masicuri (Honorato) or the Nacahuasu. There is an army report stating that they have discovered a cache of weapons in one of our camps.

At night, I got everybody together to make the following points : we are in a difficult situation; Pacho is getting better, but I am a human wreck, and the episode of the little mare proves that sometimes I have begun to lose my self-control; that will be modified, but the situation must weigh equally on everybody, and anybody who isn't able to cope must say so. It is one of those moments in which big decisions have to be taken; this type of struggle gives us the opportunity to turn ourselves into revolutionaries, the highest state of the human species, but it also allows us to graduate as men; those who are unable to reach either of these two stages must say so and quit the struggle. All the Cubans and some of the Bolivians wanted to go on to the end : Eustaquio did too, but criticized Muganga for putting his rucksack on the mule and for not carrying firewood, which provoked a hot reply from the accused. Julio attacked Moro and Pacho for much the same things and got another hot answer, this time from Pacho. I closed the discussion by saying that the two matters being debated here were in very different categories; one was whether we meant or did not mean to go on; the other was a matter of minor quarrels or internal problems in the guerrilla, which belittled such a major decision. I didn't like the complaints of Eustaquio and Julio, but equally I didn't like the replies of Moro and Pacho; in essence, we must be more revolutionary and set an example.

The eight explorers left in the morning. The machete men, Miguel, Urbano and León, got 50 minutes further away from the camp. An abscess was lanced on my heel, which allows me to put my foot down, but I feel a lot of pain and am feverish. Pacho is very well. h=780

Antonio and Chapaco went to hunt in our rear and caught a kind of deer and a turkey; they scouted at the first camp where there was nothing new and they brought along a load of oranges. I ate two of them, which immediately gave me a small attack of asthma. At 13:30 Camba arrived, one of the party of eight, with the following news: yesterday, they had to sleep without water and they had to go on until 9:00 today without finding any. Benigno recognized the place and will move towards the Rosita to find water; Pablo and Darío will come back if they do reach the water.

Fidel gave a long speech in which he attacks the traditional parties and, above all, the Venezuelan one; apparently, there has been a lot of trouble behind the scenes. They tried to cure my foot again. I'm getting better, but I am not well. Anyhow, we have to leave tomorrow to narrow the distance between our base and the machete men, who only progressed 35 minutes all day.

The trail-openers are progressing very slowly. At 16:00 Pablo and Darío came with a note from Benigno in which he announced that he was near the Rosita and that he calculated it would take three days more to get to Vargas's house. Pablito left at 8:15 from the watering place where they spent the night, and he met Miguel approximately at 15:00, which means that there is a long way to go to get there. Apparently, turkey doesn't do my asthma any good; I was given a little and had to present it to Pacho. We changed our camp to situate ourselves by a new stream which disappears by midday and reappears by midnight. It rained, but it is not cold. Many mosquitos. h=740

Grey day. The machete men advanced very little. Nothing happened here and food was short; we will sacrifice another horse tomorrow;

it will have to last for six days. My asthma has settled at a tolerable level. Barrientos announced the decline of the guerrillas and returned to menacing Cuba with an invasion; he was as stupid as always.

The radio announced a combat near Monteagudo, which resulted in the death of one of our men : Antonio Fernández from Tarata. It seems close enough to Pedro's real name; he is also from Tarata.

AUGUST 13

Miguel, Urbano, León and Camba left to camp at the watering place discovered by Benigno and to advance from there. They took with them food for three days, that is to say, chunks from Pacho's horse slaughtered today. We have four animals left, and everything seems to indicate that we will have to sacrifice another before we get more food. If everything has gone well, Coco and Aniceto should arrive here tomorrow. Arturo shot two turkeys which were apportioned to me because there is hardly any maize left. Chapaco is showing more and more signs of becoming unbalanced. Pacho is getting steadily better, but my asthma has been getting worse since yesterday; I am taking three tablets a day now. My foot is almost healed.

AUGUST 14

Black day. It was grey during our activities and there was nothing new, but there was a broadcast at night which gave the news that they had taken the cave where our party was going; the details were so precise that there can be no doubt. I am condemned to suffer from asthma now for an indeterminate time. They also captured documents of all sorts and photographs. It is the hardest blow they have inflicted on us; somebody talked. Who? We don't know that.

AUGUST 15

I sent Pablito early with a message to Miguel to send two men to look for Benigno, in case Coco and Aniceto had not yet arrived; but he met them on the way and all three came back. Miguel sent them to say that he was going to stay where night caught him and that he wanted some water brought to him. We sent Darío to warn him that we would be leaving early tomorrow morning anyway, but he ran into León returning to tell us that the path was completed.

A broadcast from Santa Cruz gave a brief report that two prisoners had been taken by the army from the Muyupampa group, which is undoubtedly Joaquín's. Our men must be badly harrassed

129

and, to top it all, those two prisoners talked. It was cold, but I did not pass a bad night; another abscess in the same foot of mine has to be lanced. Pacho is now fine.

Another clash in Chuyuyako was announced without loss by the army.

AUGUST 16

We walked effectively 3:40 hours and rested for one, along quite a good path; the mule threw me right off the saddle when pricked by a stick, but I wasn't hurt; my foot is getting better. Miguel, Urbano and Camba went on with the work of cutting and reached the Rosita. Today was the day when Benigno and his comrades should have got to the cave, and aeroplanes flew over the area several times. It could have been due to a footprint left near Vargas's house or to troops coming down the Rosita or advancing along the Grande river. At night, I warned the men about the danger of the crossing and we made careful plans for the next day.
h=600

AUGUST 17

We left early, arriving at the Rosita at 9:00. There Coco thought he heard two shots and we left an ambush, but there were no incidents. The rest of the trail went slowly, since we kept on losing and mistaking our way until we arrived at the Grande river at 16:30 and camped there. I thought we might go on by moonlight, but the men were very tired. We have rations of horsemeat for two days; for me, one day of stewed maize. It seems almost certain we will have to sacrifice another animal. The radio announced that documents and evidence will be shown, taken from the four caves by the Nacahuasu; this means that the monkeys' cave has also gone. My asthma treated me quite well, given the circumstances.
h=640 (an illogical fact, if you consider that yesterday it was 600).

AUGUST 18

We left earlier than usual, but we had to cross four fords, one of them a little deep, and we had to make trails at certain points. Because of all this, we got to the stream at 14:00 and the men dropped down to rest as if dead. There wasn't any more activity. There were clouds of flying insects in the area and it continues to be cold at night. Inti told me that Camba wants to quit; according to

130

him, his physical condition doesn't allow him to go on, and he cannot see any future in the struggle. Naturally, it is a typical case of cowardice and it would be healthy to let him go, but he already knows our future routes for trying to rejoin Joaquín and he cannot leave us. Tomorrow, I will talk with him and with Chapaco. h=680 *

AUGUST 19

Miguel, Coco, Inti and Aniceto went out to explore to try and find the best way to Vargas's house where there seems to be a detachment; but there wasn't anything new and apparently we have to follow the old path. Arturo and Chapaco went out hunting and shot a deer and the same Arturo, while on guard with Urbano, shot a tapir, which made the whole camp tense since seven shots were fired. This animal gives us meat for four days, the deer for one day, and there is a reserve of kidney beans and sardines; a total of six days' food. Apparently the white horse, the next on our list, has a chance of surviving. I talked to Camba, making it clear that he couldn't quit until our next move was fixed, which is the meeting with Joaquín. Chapaco declared that he would not quit because that would be cowardly, but he wanted the hope of getting out after six months to a year. I gave him this hope. He talked about a series of unconnected things. He is not well.

The news is full of Debray; nothing is said of the other prisoners. No news from Benigno; he could already be here.

AUGUST 20

The machete men, Miguel and Urbano, and my ' public works team ', Willy and Darío, made little progress, so we resolved to stay on the spot for another day. Coco and Inti caught nothing, but Chapaco shot a monkey and a deer. I ate some venison and it gave me a strong attack of asthma in the middle of the night. The Doctor continues to be ill, apparently with lumbago, and his general condition has turned him into an invalid. There is no news of Benigno, and from now on we have reason to feel worried.

The radio announced the presence of guerrilla fighters 85 kilometres from Sucre.

AUGUST 21

Another day in the same place and another day without news of Benigno and his comrades. Five monkeys were shot down, four by

131

Eustaquio and one by Moro as it was going by : he is still ill from
his lumbago and was given a meperidine. My asthma doesn't get on
well with the venison.

At last we made a move, but just before that, there was an alarm
because a man was seen apparently escaping along the sand-bank; it
turned out to be Urbano, who was lost. I gave a local anæsthetic to
the Doctor and with this he was able ot travel on the mare, although
he arrived in great pain; he seems a little better. Pacho made the
journey on foot. We set up camp on the right bank and we only need
a bit of machete work to prepare the trail to Vargas's house; we have
tapir meat for tomorrow and the day after, and we cannot hunt after
tomorrow. There is no news of Benigno; it is ten days since they parted
from Coco.
h=580

The day was very laborious, since we had to edge along a very bad
cliff; the white horse refused to go on, and we left it sunk in the mud
without even profiting from its bones. We reached a little hunters'
hut with traces of recent occupation; we set an ambush and soon two
men fell into it. Their excuse was that they had set ten traps and they
had gone to inspect them; according to them, the army is in Vargas's
house, in Tatarenda, Caraguatarenda, Ipitá and Yumon; two days
ago, there was a clash in Caraguatarenda with one soldier wounded.
It could be Benigno, pushed by hunger or encirclement. The men
reported that the army would come along tomorrow to fish; they come
in groups of fifteen to twenty men. We shared the tapir meat and some
fish caught with a cartridge bag; I ate rice, which suited me very well.
The Doctor is a bit better. It was announced that Debray's trial would
be postponed until September.
h=580

Reveille was set for 5:30 and we travelled to the ravine which we
thought we would follow. The advance party started the march and
had gone a few metres, when three peasants appeared on the other
side. Miguel and his men were recalled and everybody lay in ambush,
until eight soldiers appeared. I had given instructions to let them cross
the river by the ford in front of us and to fire on them when they were

reaching us, but the soldiers did not cross; they just walked up and down, passing in front of our rifles without us firing. The civilians we had captured said that they were nothing more than hunters. Miguel and Urbano, with Camba and Darío and the hunter Hugo Guzmán, were sent to follow a trail which runs towards the west, although nobody knows where it ends. We remained in ambush all the day. At nightfall, the machete men returned with the traps, which had caught a condor and a rotting cat; the whole lot ended inside us along with the last piece of the tapir; we have the kidney beans left and whatever we can hunt. Camba is reaching the last stage of moral degradation; he shivers at the mere mention of soldiers. The Doctor continues to be in pain and is being given talamonal; I am fairly well but atrociously hungry. The army issued a *communiqué* that it had taken another cave, that two of its men were slightly wounded, and that there were ' guerrilla losses '. Radio Havana gave the news of a combat in Taparillas, with one man wounded on the army's side.

AUGUST 25

The day went by without incident. Reveille was set for 5:00 and the machete men left early. Seven army men came within a few paces of our position, but they did not attempt to cross. Apparently, they are signalling the hunters with their shots; we will attack them tomorrow if we are given the opportunity. The path didn't progress far enough, since Miguel sent for Urbano to consult with him and Urbano got the message wrong, and at a time when nothing could be done.

The radio announced a combat in Monte Dorado, which seems to be under Joaquín's aegis, and the presence of guerrilla fighters at three kilometres from Camiri.

AUGUST 26

Everything went wrong: the seven men came, but they separated, five going downriver while two were crossing. Antonio, who was responsible for the ambush, fired too soon and missed, allowing the two men to escape to call up reinforcements. The other five retreated at a run. Inti and Coco fell on them in the rear, but they took cover and repelled them. While I was observing the hunt, I saw how bullets were hitting around our men, because of shooting from our own side. I went at a run and found Eustaquio shooting at them because Antonio hadn't told him anything. I was so furious that I lost control of myself and treated Antonio very roughly.

We left at a slow pace, because the Doctor cannot go fast, while the army recovered and 20 to 30 men advanced along the island in front of us; it wasn't worthwhile to face them. At a maximum, they could only have two men wounded. Coco and Inti distinguished themselves by their decisiveness.

Things went well until the Doctor became exhausted and started to hold up the march. At 18:30, we halted without reaching Miguel, who was nevertheless only a few metres ahead and made contact with us. Moro stayed in a ravine without being able to climb the last bit, and we slept divided into three groups. There are no signs of pursuit. h = 900

The day went by in a desperate search for a way out, which resulted in no clear solution as yet; we are near the Grande river and have already passed Yumon, but there are no new fords according to our information, so the only way is to go by Miguel's cliff although the mules cannot do it. We may be able to cross a small mountain chain and then continue towards the Grande river and the Masicuri, but we will only know tomorrow whether this is possible. We have crossed heights of 1,300 metres, which is approximately the maximum altitude in the zone, and we slept at 1,240 metres with the weather cold. I am very well, but the Doctor is rather ill, and the water has run out except for a little for him.

The good news, or the best thing which happened, was the appearance of Benigno, Nato and Julio. They had a long odyssey, since there are soldiers at Vargas's and Yumon, and they almost clashed with them; then they followed a troop which descended along the Saladillo and went up along the Nacahuasu; they found that the Congrí creek has three ascents made by the soldiers. The Bear cave, which they reached on the 18th, is an anti-guerrilla camp which holds about 150 soldiers; they were almost surprised there, but they managed to slip away without being seen. They were at the grandfather's *chaco,* where they picked up pumpkins — the only thing there was, since it was abandoned. They passed again through the soldiers, heard our firing and stayed to sleep nearby, so as to follow our tracks until they met up with us. According to Benigno, el Nato behaved very well, but Julio got lost twice and he was a little afraid of the soldiers. Benigno thought that some of Joaquín's men had passed by there a few days ago.

AUGUST 28

Grey day and rather anguished. We slaked our thirst with fig cakes,

134

which is more of a case of cheating the throat. Miguel sent Pablito alone with one of the hunters to look for water, and, what is more, with only a small revolver. At 16:30 he hadn't arrived and I sent Coco and Aniceto to search for him; they did not get back all night. The rear party stayed in our resting place and we couldn't hear the radio; apparently, there is a new message. In the end, we sacrificed the little mare, which has spent two hard months with us; I did everything possible to save her, but our hunger was growing and now at least we only suffer from thirst. Apparently we won't even get to the water tomorrow.

The radio gave a report of a soldier wounded in the Tatarenda area. The thing I don't know is this : if they are so scrupulous in announcing their losses, why do they lie in the rest of their reports? And if they are not lying, who are the people causing them losses in places as far apart as Caraguatarenda and Taperillas? Unless Joaquín has divided his men into two groups or there are new independent fighters.
h = 1,200

AUGUST 29

Heavy day of some anguish. The machete men made little progress and at one stage mistook the route, thinking that they were going towards the Masicuri. We made camp at an altitude of 1,600 metres in a relatively humid place which had some small cane; its pulp lessened our thirst. Some comrades, Chapaco, Eustaquio and el Chino, are becoming demoralized through lack of water. Tomorrow we will have to make straight for the closest place where we see water. The mule drivers bear up quite well.

There wasn't any big news on the radio; the most interesting is Debray's trial, which stretches out from one week to the next.

AUGUST 30

The situation became agonizing; the machete men were fainting, Miguel and Darío were drinking their own urine, and so was el Chino, and the horrible results were diarrhœa and cramps. Urbano, Benigno and Julio descended into a canyon and found water. They warned me that the mules couldn't get down, and I decided to stay with el Nato, but Inti came up again with water and the three of us remained, eating the mare. The radio stayed below so that there wasn't any news.
h = 1,200

Aniceto and León went exploring in the morning down below, and they came back at 16:00 hours with the news that there was a way to take the mules from the camp to the water in front. The worst stage was the first, but I looked at it and the animals can get through. So I ordered Miguel to make a short cut for us tomorrow on the last cliff and to go on opening the trail in front, so that we can get the mules down. There is a message from Manila, but we could not record it.

ANALYSIS OF THE MONTH
Beyond a doubt, it was the worst month we have had from the point of view of the war. The loss of all the caves with their documents and medicines was a hard blow, above all psychologically. The loss of two men in the last days of the month and the subsequent march on horsemeat demoralized the men, provoking the first case of quitting, Camba's; at all other times this would be a net gain, but not in the present circumstances. The lack of contact with the outside world and with Joaquín, and the fact that some of his men have talked after capture, has also demoralized the group a little. My sickness spread doubt in some more and all of this was reflected in our only skirmish, in which we should have caused the enemy some losses instead of only one wounded. Not only that, but the difficult march through the hills without water brought out some negative angles in the men.

The most important characteristics are:

(1) We continue without any sort of contacts and without any reasonable hope of establishing them in the near future.

(2) We continue without incorporating the peasants, a logical thing indeed, if the little contact we have had with them lately is considered.

(3) There is a decline, I hope only temporary, in our fighting morale.

(4) The army is not increasing its effectiveness nor its fighting power.

We are at a low moment in our morale and in the legend of the revolution. The most urgent tasks continue to be the same as in the previous month: these are, to re-establish contacts, recruit combatants, stock up medicines and equipment.

One thing must be considered, that Inti and Coco show themselves every time firmer and firmer as revolutionary and military commissars.

SEPTEMBER, 1967

We got the mules down early, after some mishaps which included a spectacular tumble into the depths by the male one. The Doctor has not recovered, but I am better and walk perfectly leading the mule. The way stretched out more than we thought, and not until 18:15 did we realize that we were at the stream by Honorato's house. Miguel went on at full speed, but he only got to the main road by the time it was already dark. Benigno and Urbano advanced cautiously and did not notice anything abnormal; so they occupied the house which had been vacated, although the army had added some barrack rooms to it, which were abandoned for the moment. We found flour, lard, salt and goats, two of which we killed; they made a real feast along with the flour, although the whole night was taken up in waiting for it to cook. At dawn we withdrew, leaving a sentry in the little house and at the road entrance.
h=740

Early in the morning, we retired to the *chacos,* leaving an ambush in the house in charge of Miguel with Coco, Pablo and Benigno. A sentry was posted on the other side. At eight o'clock, Coco came to warn us that a mule driver had passed by looking for Honorato; there were four in all and he was ordered to let the other three pass. All this news came late, since it took an hour to get from our point to the house. At 13:30 some shots were heard and then we learned that a peasant was coming along with a soldier and a horse. El Chino, who was doing sentry duty with Pombo and Eustaquio, shouted: A soldier. He cocked his rifle, and the soldier shot at him and fled away, while Pombo fired and killed the horse. My rage was spectacular, as this was the nadir of incompetence; poor el Chino was overwhelmed. We released the four men, who had passed through in the interim, as well as our two prisoners, and we sent everybody up the Masicuri. We bought a bullock from the mule drivers for 700 pesos and Hugo was given 100 pesos for his work and 50 pesos for certain things taken from him. The dead horse turned out to be one that had been left at Honorato's house because it was lame. The mule drivers said that Honorato's wife had complained about the army for beating her husband and for eating up everything she had. When the mule drivers went past eight days ago, Honorato was in Vallegrande recovering from a wildcat bite. Anyhow, somebody had been in the house, since we found a lighted fire when we arrived. Owing to el Chino's mistake, I decided to leave at night in the same direction as the mule drivers and to try to get to the first house, presuming that there were few soldiers and they had continued their retreat; but we left very late and we only crossed the ford at 3:45 without finding the house and we slept on a cow-path to wait for daybreak.

There was some ugly news on the radio about the annihilation of a group of ten men led by a Cuban called Joaquín in the Camiri area. The broadcast, however, came from the Voice of America and the local stations haven't said anything.

SEPTEMBER 3

As happens on Sundays, there was a clash. At dawn, we explored down the Masicuri as far as its outlet and then we went some way up the Grande river. At 13:00 hours, Inti, Coco, Benigno, Pablito, Julio and León went off to try and reach the house, if the army wasn't there, and to buy some goods to make our life more bearable. Firstly, the group captured two peons who said the owner wasn't about, there were no soldiers, and they could get hold of quite a lot of food. Other reports : five soldiers had passed at the gallop without halting at the house; Honorato went by two days ago going towards his house with two of his sons. As our men reached the house of the land-owner, they met 40 soldiers who had just arrived; there was a con-fusing encounter in which our men killed at least one soldier who was leading a dog; the soldiers reacted by surrounding them, but later retreated because of shouting; not even a grain of rice could be picked up. The aeroplane flew over the area and shot some rockets, apparently by the Nacahuasu. Other reports from the peasants : no guerrilla fighters have been seen in this area and the first information they had was from the mule drivers who passed through yesterday.

The Voice of America again gave some information about clashes with the army, and this time it named José Carrillo as the only survivor of the group of ten. As this Carrillo is Paco, one of the feeble ones, and as the annihilation supposedly took place by the Masicuri, everything seems to indicate that it is a whopping lie.
h=650

SEPTEMBER 4

A group of eight men, commanded by Miguel, set an ambush on the road from the Masicuri to Honorato's until 13:00 hours without incident. Meanwhile, el Nato and Léon brought in a cow after much

138

labour, but later two magnificent tame oxen were secured. Urbano and Camba travelled some ten kilometres upriver; they had to cross four fords, one of which was rather deep. The bullock was killed and volunteers were asked for, to make an excursion in search of food and information; Inti, Coco, Julio, Aniceto, Chapaco and Arturo were sent off under Inti; Pacho, Pombo, Antonio and Eustaquio also volunteered. Inti's instructions are : to arrive at dawn at the house, to observe all movements, and to get supplies if there are no soldiers; to go round the house and move forwards, if there are soldiers; to try and capture one, remembering that the fundamental thing is not to have any losses; the utmost caution is recommended.

The radio brought the news of a death in Vado del Yeso, near where the group of ten men was liquidated; this was in a new clash, which makes the story about Joaquín seem false. On the other hand, they gave full details about el Negro and the Peruvian doctor, who died in Palmarito and was transferred to Camiri; el Pelado collaborated in his identification. Apparently, this is a real death; the other ones may be fictitious or be the feeble ones in the group. Anyhow, there is a strange flavour in the reports, which are now transferred to the Masicuri and Camiri.

SEPTEMBER 5

The day went by with nothing new happening, while we waited for the result. At 4:30 the group returned, bringing a mule and some goods. There were soldiers at the house of the landowner, Morón; these were on the point of discovering our group through their dogs; apparently, they move at night. Our men went round the house and cut through the woods as far as Montaño's house, where there was nobody, but yes, there was maize, of which a quintal was brought along. At noon approximately, they crossed the river and fell on the two houses that happened to be on the other side. Everyone escaped from one of them and they requisitioned the mule there; in the other house, there was very little collaboration and threats had to be used. The reports we were given were that no guerrilla fighters had been seen up till then, and only one group (us) had gone by Pérez's house before the carnival. They returned by day and waited for night to bypass Morón's house. Everything was going perfectly, but Arturo lost his way and went to sleep on the path, so two hours were wasted looking for him; some tracks were left that could be traced if the cattle don't wipe them out; moreover, certain things were dropped by the wayside. The men's spirits changed immediately.

139

The radio reported that the dead guerrilla fighters could not be identified, but there might be new developments at any moment. We deciphered all of a message saying that OLAS was a triumph, but that the Bolivian delegation was a shitty lot; Aldo Flores from the Bolivian Communist Party pretended that he was the representative of the Army of National Liberation; he had to be proved a liar. One of Kolle's men has been asked to go for a discussion. Lozano's house has been raided and he has gone underground; he thinks that there could be an exchange for Debray. That is all; evidently, they have not yet received our last message.

Benigno   SEPTEMBER 6

Benigno's birthday had a promising start : in the early morning, we made corn meal with what had been brought and we drank a little *maté* with sugar. Later Miguel, in command of eight more men, set an ambush, while León collected another bullock to take away. As it was a bit late, after 10:00, and they had not come back, I sent Urbano to warn them to call off the ambush by 12:00. A few minutes later, a shot was heard, then a short burst of fire and a shot in our direction. As we were taking up our positions, Urbano arrived at a run; he had clashed with a dog patrol. I was in utter despair because I did not know the precise location of my nine men on the other side. The path was improved to take it to the river bank without coming out there, and Moro, Pombo and Camba with Coco were sent down it. I thought of transferring the rucksacks and keeping in contact with the rear party, if allowed, until they were incorporated again in the group, which might then fall into an ambush. Miguel, however, rejoined us with all his men, cutting his way through the forest.

Explanation of what happened : Miguel advanced without leaving a sentry on our little path and concentrated on looking for cattle; León heard the barking of a dog and Miguel was uneasy enough to decide to retreat; at that moment, they heard the shots and realized that a patrol had passed along a track between them and the forest, and was already ahead of them; so they cut their way back through the forest.

We withdrew without difficulty, taking the three mules and the three head of cattle; we crossed four fords, two of them difficult, then camped about seven kilometres further on, and sacrificed the cow to have a feast. The rear party reported that it heard a long burst of shooting in the direction of our camp with a lot of machine-gun fire. h=640

Short journey. We crossed only one ford and then ran into difficulties because of a cliff; so Miguel decided to make camp and wait. Tomorrow we will explore thoroughly. The situation is this : the air force is not looking for us here in spite of reaching our camp, and the radio reports include the fact that I am head of the group. The question is : Are they afraid? Not likely. Or do they consider the way up to here impossible? With the experience of what we have done and what they know, I don't think so. Are they letting us advance to wait for us at a strategic point? It's possible. Do they think we will have to go to the Masicuri area for our supplies? It's also possible. The Doctor is much better, but I am beginning to get worse and spent a night without sleep.

The radio brings news of the valuable information given by José Carrillo (Paco); we will have to make an example of him. Debray referred to Paco's accusations of him, saying that he had gone hunting from time to time, which is why he was seen with a gun. Radio Cruz del Sur announced the finding of the body of the guerrilla fighter Tania on the banks of the Grande river; the news doesn't sound as authentic as the news about el Negro. According to this radio station, the body was taken to Santa Cruz, but not according to the Altiplano station.

I talked to Julio; he is fine, but he feels the lack of contact and of the recruitment of more people.
h=720

Quiet day. We set ambushes of eight men from morning until night under the command of Antonio and Pombo. The animals had a good meal in a field of bamboo and the mule is recovering from its beating. Aniceto and Chapaco went to explore upriver and returned with the news that the path was quite good for the animals; Coco and Camba crossed the river with water up to their chests and climbed a hill in front, but they did not get any information from it. I sent Miguel off with Aniceto, and the result of their more prolonged exploration is that, according to Miguel, it will be very difficult to get the animals through. We will stick to this side tomorrow, because there is always the possibility of the animals getting through without loads and by water.

The radio brought the news that Barrientos had been present at the

funeral of the remains of the guerrilla fighter Tania, who was given
a ' Christian burial '; later he went to Puerto Mauricio, which is
Honorato's house. He has made a proposition to all the deluded
Bolivians, whose promised bribes have not been paid; if they present
themselves with their hands up at any army post, no measures will be
taken against them. A little aeroplane dropped bombs from Honorato's on down, just to make a demonstration for Barrientos.

A Budapest newspaper criticizes Che Guevara as a pathetic and
apparently irresponsible figure, and it hails the Marxist attitude of the
Chilean Party which takes up practical attitudes when faced with
reality. How I would like to get to power, only to strip the mask off
cowards and lackeys of all sorts and to rub their noses in their own
filthy tricks.

SEPTEMBER 9

Miguel and el Nato went to explore, coming back with the news that
we can cross, but that the animals will have to swim for it; the men
will have fords. There is quite a big stream on the left bank where
we will camp. We still set the eight-man ambushes with Antonio and
Pombo in charge; there was nothing new. I spoke to Aniceto; he
seems very steady, although he thinks some of the Bolivians are
weakening; he complains about the lack of political work by Coco
and Inti. We finished the cow; only its four legs are left for a broth
in the morning.

The only news on the radio is the suspension of Debray's trial
until the 17th of September, at the least.

SEPTEMBER 10

Bad day. It began beneath good auspices, but then the animals baulked
at so bad a road and finally the male mule would not move at all. It
stayed behind and had to be left on the other bank; Coco took this
decision owing to a violent rise in the river; but four weapons had
been left on the other side, including Moro's and three anti-tank shells
for Benigno's. I crossed the river swimming with the mule, but I lost
my shoes during the crossing, and now I am in sandals, something
which does not please me at all. El Nato made a bundle of his clothes
and weapons, wrapping them in plastic, and plunged in when the
flood was rising, and lost everything on the way. The other mule got
stuck and began to cross alone, but it had to be taken back because
there was no passage for it, and when it was crossing again with León,
they both nearly drowned because of the rush of water. In the end,

142

we all reached the stream which was our goal; the Doctor was in a very bad way and later complained all night long of neuralgia in his extremities. From here, our plan was to make the animals swim again to the other bank, but the floods have interrupted this plan, at least until the river has gone down. In addition, aeroplanes and helicopters have flown over the area; I did not like the helicopter at all, as it could mean that they are setting ambushes for us along the river. We will scout upriver and upstream tomorrow, to try and find out precisely where we are.

I almost forgot to emphasize one fact : after something more than six months, I had a bath today. It constitutes a record which some of the others are already approaching.

h = 780.   Distance = 3-4 kilometres.

SEPTEMBER 11

Quiet day. The scouts went upriver and upstream; the river scouts came back in the evening with the news that there would very probably be a way by the river when it went down some more, and that there were beaches on which the beasts can walk. Benigno and Julio went to scout up the stream, but they did it very superficially and were back by 12:00. El Nato and Coco went, supported by the rear party, to fetch the things left behind; they got the mule across and only left behind a sack containing the belts of machine-gun bullets.

There was one unpleasant incident : el Chino came to tell me that el Nato had roasted and eaten a whole fillet of meat in his presence. I was angry with el Chino because it was his duty to stop this, but after investigation, things became complicated because it was impossible to be certain whether el Chino had authorized the action or not. He asked to be replaced and I named Pombo again to the command; but above all, it was a bitter pill for el Chino to swallow.

In the morning the radio brought the news that Barrientos has claimed I have been dead for some time and everything was propaganda; in the evening, he offered 50,000 pesos (4,200 U.S. dollars) for details leading to my capture, dead or alive. Apparently, the armed forces gave him a [———][1]. They had probably dropped leaflets over the region, giving particulars about me. Requeterán says that Barrientos' offer can be considered a psychological one, as they already know how tenacious guerrilla fighters are, and as they are preparing for a long war.

---

[1] Illegible in the original.

I had a long talk with Pablito, who is worried, like the rest of us, by the lack of contact, and who feels that our primary task is to re-establish ties with the city. However, he showed himself to be firm and full of determination to stay with us, ' de Patria o Muerte ', until the end.

The day began with a tragi-comic episode : at 6:00 precisely, time for reveille, Eustaquio came to warn us that some men were advancing along the stream; he called us to arms and everybody mobilized. Antonio had seen them and when I asked how many there were of them, he held up his fingers to show there were five. In fact, it turned out to be a hallucination, dangerous for the morale of the troop as the men immediately started to talk of psychosis. Later, I talked to Antonio and evidently he wasn't normal; tears came to his eyes, but he denied that there was anything on his mind and said that he is only affected by lack of sleep, because he has had six days' extra duty for falling asleep at his post and then for denying it. Chapaco disobeyed an order and was punished by three days' extra duty. At night, he asked to be transferred to the advance party because he said he did not get on with Antonio; I denied his request. Inti, León and Eustaquio set off to make a thorough exploration of the stream to see if we can use it to cross to the other side of a big mountain range we can see in the distance. Coco, Aniceto and Julio went upriver to try and explore the fords and the method of taking the animals with us in case we go by that way.

Apparently, Barrientos' offer has provoked a small sensation. In any case, a mad journalist thought that 4,200 dollars wasn't much considering how dangerous I was. Radio Havana reported that OLAS had received a message of support from the Army of National Liberation. A miracle of telepathy by me !

The explorers returned : Inti and his group climbed up by the stream all day. They slept at quite a high altitude, also rather cold; the stream apparently springs from a mountain range to the front of us and to the west; it cannot be crossed by the animals. Coco and his comrades tried unsuccessfully to cross the river; they traversed eleven cliffs before coming to a canyon which must be that of the Pesca river. It had signs of life with burned *chacos* and an ox. The animals will have to cross to the other side, unless we all make a raft to go together,

144

which is what we will try to do.

I spoke with Darío, putting to him the question of his departure, if he wants to leave; at first, he replied that it was very dangerous to go. But I warned him that this was not a place of refuge, and that if he decided to stay, it was once and for all. He said that he would stay and he would correct his defects. We will see.

The only news on the radio was that a warning shot had been fired at Debray's father and that all the documents prepared by his son for his defence had been taken away, under the pretext that they don't want these to be turned into a political pamphlet.

SEPTEMBER 14

Fatiguing day. At 7:00 Miguel left with all the advance party and el Nato. They had instructions to travel as far as they could along this bank and to make a raft when it became difficult to get through; Antonio stayed with all the rear party in ambush. A pair of M-1's were left in a little cave which el Nato and Willy know. At 3:30 we began to march, since we had no news.

We couldn't travel on mule-back, and I had to leave the animal to León and follow on foot, although I was at the beginning of an asthma attack. The rear party received the order to start marching at 15:00, if there wasn't a counter-order. Approximately at that hour, Pablito arrived with the news that the ox had reached the place for the animals' crossing and that the raft was being built one kilometre further up. I waited for the animals to arrive and they only did so by 18:15, after the men had been sent to help them. At that hour, the two mules crossed (the ox had already done so beforehand) and we proceeded at a slow pace to where the raft was, to find that there were still twelve men remaining on this side; only ten had got across. Thus we spent the night divided, eating the last ration of half-rotten beef. h=720.   Distance=2-3 kilometres.

SEPTEMBER 15

The stretch we covered was a little longer : five to six kilometres, although we did not reach the Pesca river, for we had to make the animals cross twice over, and one of the mules baulked at the crossings. We still have to cross once more and scout to see if the mules can do it.

The radio brings the news of Loyola's arrest. The photographs must be to blame for it. The only bull we had left died, in the executioner's hands, of course.

h=780

145

The whole day was spent in making the raft and crossing the river, so we only travelled some 500 metres as far as the camp where there is a little spring. The crossing was made without incident on a good raft, which was pulled by ropes from both banks. In the end, when they were left alone, Antonio and Chapaco had another quarrel and Antonio gave Chapaco six days' punishment for insulting him; I stood by his decision, although I am not sure it is just. At night, there was another incident because Eustaquio denounced el Nato for eating an extra meal; it turned out to be some fat bits on the hides. Another painful situation caused by food. The Doctor gave me another little problem; it was about his sickness and about what the men thought of it, after certain remarks made by Julio. All of this seems unimportant.

h=820

Pablito
Dental surgery day; I pulled teeth from Arturo and Chapaco. Miguel explored up to the river and Benigno the path; they reported that the mules could get up, but before that, they would have to swim across the river both ways. In honour of Pablito, a little rice was prepared for him; he is twenty-two today and the baby of the guerrilla.

The radio only brought news of the postponement of the trial and a protest against the detention of Loyola Guzmán.

The march began at 7:00, but Miguel soon came with the news that three peasants had been seen round the bend; he didn't know if they had seen us, but orders were given to detain them. Inevitably, Chapaco picked a quarrel, accusing Arturo of having stolen fifteen bullets from his magazine; he is vicious and the only good thing is that, although his quarrels are with the Cubans, the Bolivians don't pay any attention to him. The mules managed the whole journey without having to swim, but the black mule slipped and injured itself while crossing a gorge, since it rolled over for about 50 metres. Four peasants were taken prisoner as they were going with their little donkeys to the Piraypandi, a river situated a league from here upstream, and they reported that Aladino Gutiérrez and his men were hunting and fishing on the banks of the Grande river. Benigno committed the rash act of letting himself be seen and then allowing Aladino, his wife and another peasant to go. When I heard of this, I was livid with rage and called this an act of treason, which provoked a storm of weeping from Benigno. All the peasants have been warned that they will have to leave with us to Zitano, the settlement where they live some six to eight leagues from here. Aladino and his wife are rather sly and it cost a lot to get food from them. The radio now brings news of two suicide attempts by Loyola ' for fear of reprisals by the guerrillas ' and the arrest of some teachers, who may not be involved with us, but at least show sympathy for us. Apparently, they took a great deal from Loyola's house, but it would not surprise me if it was all the result of the photographs from the cave.

In the evening, the little aeroplane and a Mustang flew over the area in a suspicious way.

h = 800

<small>SEPTEMBER</small> 19

We didn't leave very early because the peasants couldn't find their beasts. In the end, after I'd given them a good lecture, we left with the caravan of prisoners. What with Moro, we walked slowly and when we had to turn away from the river, we were met with the news that three more prisoners had been taken, and that the advance party had just left and expected to reach a cane plantation two leagues further on. They were long leagues, just as overlong as the first two ones. About nine o'clock at night we got to the plantation, which is only one field. The rear party arrived after 21:00.

I had a conversation with Inti about some weaknesses of his over food, and he was quite annoyed when he answered me to say that he would make a public self-criticism when we were by ourselves, but he did deny certain of the accusations. We crossed heights of 1,440 metres and we are now at 1,000 metres; it is three hours' march from here to Lucitano, or perhaps four according to the pessimists. At last we had some pork to eat and those with a sweet tooth could fill themselves with molasses cake.

The radio kept on about the Loyola case and the teachers are out on strike. The pupils are on hunger strike at the secondary school where Higueras, one of the arrested men, worked, and the oil workers are about to strike because of the formation of the big oil enterprise.

Sign of the times : I've finished all the ink.

<small>SEPTEMBER</small> 20

I decided to leave at 15:00 to arrive at the Lucitano settlement at dusk, since they said we would get there within three hours, but various

147

hold-ups delayed our journey until 17:00, and we were caught by total darkness on the hill. In spite of that, we lit a lamp and only got to Aladino Gutiérrez's house at 23:00. It wasn't much of a general store, although we got some cigars and other trifles; no clothes at all. We snatched some sleep before starting the march at 3:00 towards Alto Seco, which they say is four leagues away. We took the magistrate's telephone, but it hasn't been working for years and the line has also fallen down. The magistrate is called Vargas and he has only been in office for a little while.

The radio broadcast nothing important; we crossed heights of 1,800 metres while Lucitano is at 1,400 metres.

We had to walk about two leagues to reach the settlement.

SEPTEMBER 21

At 3:00, we left under a good moon on a trail indicated to us beforehand, and we walked until approximately 9:00 without meeting a soul and crossing heights of 2,040 metres, the greatest we have reached. At that hour we came across a couple of mule drivers who pointed out the way to Alto Seco, still two leagues away; it had taken us part of the night and the morning to travel only two leagues. When we got to the first houses on the way down, we bought some food and went to the mayor's house to make our meal. Later, we passed by a corn mill run by hydraulic power on the banks of the Piraymiri (1,400 metres altitude). The people are very frightened and try to disappear at our coming; we have lost a lot of time due to our limited mobility. It took from 12:35 until 17:00 to make the two leagues to Alto Seco.

SEPTEMBER 22

When we in the centre party came to Alto Seco, we found out that the magistrate had apparently gone out yesterday to warn that we were nearby; as a reprisal, we took everything in his general store. Alto Seco is a little village of 50 houses, situated at 1,900 metres altitude; it received us with a good mixture of fear spiced with curiosity. The supply machinery began to work and we soon had a respectable amount of food in our camp, an abandoned house near the watering place. The small truck which ought to have arrived from Vallegrande did not do so, which confirmed the story that the magistrate had left to give warning; all the same, I had to put up with the weeping of his wife who, in the name of God and her children, asked to be paid, something I refused to do. At night, Inti gave a talk in the local school (1st and 2nd Grades) to a group of fifteen amazed and silent peasants,

148

explaining to them the extent of our revolution. The teacher was the only one who interrupted to ask if we fought in villages. He is a mixture of foxy peasant and literate man, with the ingenuity of a child; he asked a mass of things about socialism. A big boy offered to be our guide, but he warned us against the teacher who is said to be a fox. We left at 1:30 in the direction of Santa Elena where we arrived at 10:00.

Barrientos and Ovando gave a press conference at which they gave out all the data from the documents and declared that Joaquín's group was liquidated.
h = 1,300

SEPTEMBER 23
The place was a very beautiful orange grove which still has a large quantity of fruit. We spent the day resting and sleeping, but we had to post many sentries. At 1:00 we rose, and went at 2:00 in the direction of Loma Larga, which we reached at dawn. We crossed heights of 1,800 metres. The men were carrying a lot and the march went slowly. I got indigestion from the meal made by Benigno.

SEPTEMBER 24
We reached the settlement called Loma Larga; I had a liver upset and vomited. The men are very tired from the long marches which don't result in anything. I decided to spend the night at the fork of the road to Pujio, and we killed a pig sold to us by Sóstenos Vargas, the only peasant who stayed in his house. The rest flee at the sight of us.
h = 1,400

SEPTEMBER 25
We arrived at Pujio early, but there were people there who had seen us below the day before, which means to say that news of us is being broadcast by word of mouth. Pujio is a little settlement situated on a height, and the people, who fled at the sight of us, later came near us and treated us well. Very early in the morning, a rural policeman had left; he had come to arrest a debtor from Serrano in Chuquisaca; we are at a point where the three departments converge. Travelling with mules is becoming dangerous, but I am trying to keep the Doctor as well as possible, for he is still weak. The peasants say they haven't seen the army in this area. We walked in stages until we reached Tranca Mayo where we slept at the side of the road, since Miguel

149

did not take the precautions required by me. The magistrate from Higueras is in the area and I gave the sentry the order to detain him.

Inti and I spoke to Camba and he agreed to accompany us as far as la Higuera, a point situated near Pucará; from there, he would try to leave for Santa Cruz.

h = 1,800

SEPTEMBER 26

Defeat. At dawn we arrived at Picacho where everybody was having a fiesta and which was the highest point we had reached, 2,280 metres. The peasants treated us very well and we went on without much concern, although Ovando had guaranteed my capture from one moment to another. Everything changed with our arrival in la Higuera: all the men had disappeared and there were only a few women. Coco went to the telegraphist's house, because there was a telephone, and he found a message dated the 2nd in which the sub-prefect of Vallegrande told the magistrate that he should note the presence of guerrillas in the area and that any news of them whatever should be communicated to Vallegrande which would pay for the costs. The man had fled; but his wife assured us that nobody had spoken on the telephone today as there was a fiesta in the next town, Jagüey.

At 13:00 the advance party left to try to reach Jagüey and to take a decision there about the mules and the Doctor; a little afterwards, I was talking with the only man left in the village, and very frightened too, when a coca trader arrived, saying that he had come from Vallegrande and Pucará and had seen nothing. He was also very nervous, but he put it down to our presence, and I let them both go in spite of the lies they had told us. When I left towards the peak of the hill at 13:30 approximately, shots from everywhere on the ridge announced that our men had fallen into an ambush. I organized our defence in the village, to wait for the survivors and to fix on a way out along a trail leading to the Grande river. After a few moments, the wounded Benigno appeared and then Aniceto and Pablito with his foot in a bad mess; Miguel, Coco and Julio had fallen and Camba had disappeared, leaving his rucksack. The rear party advanced down the trail rapidly and I followed it, still leading the two mules; those in the rear were shot at from nearby and they withdrew and Inti lost contact with us. After waiting for him for half an hour in a little ambush and having taken more fire from the hill, we decided to leave him, but a little later he came up to us. At that moment, we saw that León had disappeared and Inti told us that he had seen his rucksack

150

in the defile through which he had got out; we saw a man travelling fast along a canyon and came to the conclusion that it was him. To try to throw them off our tracks, we loosed the mules down the canyon and we went on by a little canyon which held some bitter water further on. We slept at midnight, since it was impossible to advance.

At 4:00 we started to march again, trying to find a place to climb out, something which we managed to do by 7:00, but not on the side we wanted; there was a barren hill in front of us which looked harmless. We climbed a little more to be safeguarded from the air in a sparse little wood, and there we found that the hill had a path on it, although nobody used it all day. At nightfall, a peasant and a soldier climbed halfway up the hill and spent a bit of time there, without seeing us. Aniceto had just finished scouting and had seen quite a big group of soldiers in a nearby house; that was the easiest way for us to go and it is cut off now. In the morning, we saw a column on a hill nearby; its equipment shone in the sun as it climbed; and then at noon, we heard isolated shots and bursts of machine-gun fire and later shouts of : ' There he is '; ' Out of there '; ' Are you coming out or not '; together with some shots. We don't know what happened to the man and we presume that it might be Camba. We went out in the evening to try to get down to the water on the other side and we remained in a thicket a little denser than the previous one. We had to look for water in the canyon itself, because a cliff did not allow us to do it here.

The radio carried the news that we had clashed with the Galindo company, leaving three men dead who were going to be transferred to Vallegrande for identification. Apparently, they haven't captured Camba and León. Our losses have been very great this time; Coco's loss was the worst to bear of these, but Miguel and Julio were magnificent fighters and the human value of all three was more than I can say. León was shaping well.
h = 1,400

Day of anxieties; at one moment, it looked like our last one. At dawn, some water was brought, and Inti and Willy left almost at once to scout for another possible descent to the canyon; but they soon came back, because a trail winds right across the hill in front and a peasant on horseback was travelling along it. At 10:00, 46 soldiers passed in

151

front of us with their rucksacks, taking ages to go away. At 12:00, another group made its appearance, this time numbering 77 men; to top it all, a shot was heard at that moment and the soldiers took up their positions; their officer ordered them down into the ravine, which looked like ours anyhow. In the end, however, he got a radio message which seemed to satisfy him, and he started the march again. Our hiding-place had no defence against an attack from above and our possibilities of escaping were remote, if they had discovered us. A soldier who had fallen back passed by later with a tired dog, which had to be pulled along to make it walk, and even later, another little lagging soldier came past guided by a peasant. The peasant returned after a while and there was nothing new; but our anxiety at the moment of the shot was great. All the soldiers were going by with their rucksacks, which gave the impression that they were withdrawing, and no fires were seen in the little house at night, nor were any of the shots heard which are usually fired to greet nightfall. Tomorrow, we will scout all day around the settlement. A light rain made us damp, but I don't think it was enough to wipe out our tracks.

The radio gave the news of Coco's identification and confusing news about Julio; Miguel has been mistaken for Antonio, whose position in Manila was given. At the beginning, they announced the news of my death, then they retracted it.

SEPTEMBER 29

Another tense day. Inti and Aniceto went out to scout early and to watch the house for the whole day. From early morning onwards, people used the path and by mid-morning, soldiers without their rucksacks were using it in both directions, while others led unloaded donkeys down below, which then returned loaded. Inti arrived at 18:15 to report that the sixteen soldiers who descended went into the *chaco* and could not be seen again, and that the donkeys seemed to have been loaded there. Given these reports, it is difficult to take the decision to use this trail, the easiest and most logical one, since there may well be soldiers in ambush on it and, in any case, there are dogs in the house which will signal our passing. Two scouting trips will be made tomorrow; one to the same place and the other to try to travel up the ridge as far as possible to see if there is a way out by there, probably crossing the road that the soldiers take.

The radio didn't give any news.

Another day of tension. In the morning, Radio Balmaceda of Chile announced that highly-placed army sources had declared that they had Che Guevara corralled in a wooded canyon. Local radio stations are silent; apparently, the news could be *treason* and they are certain that we are here in the area. After a short while, the movement of the soldiers from one side to the other started. At noon, 40 passed by in separate columns with their weapons at the ready, and they went to the little house where they camped and nervously posted sentries. Aniceto and Pacho reported this. Inti and Willy came back with the news that the Grande river is about two kilometres away in a straight line, that there are three houses further up the canyon, and that we can camp in places where we will not be seen from any side. We fetched water and began a tiring night march at 22:00, held back by el Chino who travels very badly in the darkness. Benigno is very well, but the Doctor has never recovered completely.

Analysis of the Month

It should have been a month of recuperation and it almost was, when Miguel, Coco and Julio fell into an ambush, which spoiled everything, and since then we have remained in a dangerous position, also losing León; Camba's loss is a definite gain.

We had small skirmishes in which we killed a horse, killed and wounded a soldier, and Urbano exchanged shots with a patrol; then the nefarious ambush of la Higuera. We have already given up the mules, and I think that it will be a long time before we have animals of that type again, except if I fall back into a bad asthma attack.

On the other hand, some of the news about deaths in the other group seems to be true, so that we ought to consider it liquidated, although a small group of them may possibly be wandering about, avoiding contact with the army, because the news of the death of seven of them together can be false or, at least, exaggerated.

The characteristics are the same as in the past month, except that the army is now showing itself more effective in action, and the peasant mass aids us in nothing and is turning into informers.

The most important task is to break out and seek for more suitable areas; then the contacts, in spite of the fact that all the apparatus is wrecked in La Paz where we have also been given some hard knocks. The morale of the rest of the men has kept up quite well, and I only have my doubts about Willy, who may take advantage of some scuffle to try and escape on his own, if I don't talk to him about it.

153

OCTOBER, 1967

The first day of the month passed with no incidents.

At dawn, we arrived at a small sparse wood where we camped, placing sentries at the different points of approach. The 40 men went away down the canyon we were thinking of taking; they fired some shots. At 14:00, we heard the last shots; nobody seems to be in the little houses, although Urbano saw five soldiers come down, not following any trail. I decided to stay here one more day, because the place is good and has a guaranteed way of retreat, since we overlook almost all the movements of the enemy troops. Pacho, with el Nato, Darío and Eustaquio, went to fetch water and returned at 21:00. Chapaco cooked some fritters and we had a little *charqui* which made us forget our hunger.

There was no news.

h = 1,600

Antonio   OCTOBER 2

The day went by without any trace of the soldiers, but sheepdogs chivvied some little goats past our positions and the animals barked. We decided to bypass one of the *chacos* that is nearer to the canyon and we began the descent at 18:00; we easily had the time to arrive and cook before we crossed, except that el Nato lost himself and obstinately wanted to go on. When we decided to retreat, we got lost and had to spend the night on the height without being able to cook and very thirsty. The radio brought us the explanation of the deployment of the soldiers on the 30th; according to a broadcast on the Cruz del Sur, the army reported having a skirmish in the Quiñol gorge with a small group of ours; there were no casualties on either side, although they said they had found traces of blood after our flight. According to the same source the group was composed of six individuals.

OCTOBER 3

A long and unnecessarily intense day : when we mobilized to get to our base camp, Urbano came with the news that he had heard some peasants pass by and comment : ' Those are the ones who were talking last night ', while we were on our way. Clearly, the report was inaccurate, but I decided to act as if it were perfectly realistic and, without satisfying our thirst, we climbed again to a ridge which dominated the soldiers' trail. The rest of the day passed in absolute calm and in the

154

evening we all descended and made coffee, which tasted glorious in spite of the bitter water and the grease from the kettle in which it was made. Then we prepared maize flour to eat there and rice with tapir meat to take with us. At 3:00 we started marching after scouting first and we happily crossed the *chaco,* reaching the selected ravine, which has no water and shows signs of having been searched by the soldiers.

The radio brought the news of two prisoners: Antonio Domínguez Flores (León) and Orlando Jiménez Bazán (Camba), who admits to fighting against the army; León says he surrendered, trusting the presidential word. Both gave a lot of news about Fernando, about my sickness and all the rest, without counting what they must have said off the record. So ends the story of two heroic guerrilla fighters.

We heard an interview with Debray, very bravely confronting a student who provoked him.
h=1,360

OCTOBER 4

After resting in the ravine, we followed it for half an hour downwards, until we found another one that joined it; we climbed that and rested until 15:00 to avoid the sun. We then began to march again for a little more than half an hour. There we reached the scouts who had got to the ends of the little canyons without finding water. At 18:00 we abandoned the ravine and followed a cattle track until 19:30, an hour when visibility was nil, and we halted until 3:00.

The radio gave the news of the change of the forward HQ of the General Staff of the 4th Division from Lagunillas to Padilla, in order to concentrate more on the Serrano area where the guerrilla fighters might presumably try to escape. The commentator thinks that if I am captured by forces of the 4th, I will be tried in Camiri; if it is done by those of the 8th, it will be Santa Cruz.
h=1,650

OCTOBER 5

When we started the march again, we travelled with difficulty until 5:15 hours, the time when we left the cattle track and went into a sparse thicket, sufficiently tall to cover us from indiscreet eyes. Benigno and Pacho made several scouting trips looking for water and went completely around the house nearby without finding any; there is probably a little well beside it. At the end of the expedition, they saw six soldiers arrive at the house, apparently from the trail. We left in the evening with the men exhausted because of the lack of water, and

155

Eustaquio made a scene and cried for a mouthful of water. After a very bad trail which made us stop several times, we arrived at a little wood at dawn from where we could hear the barking of dogs nearby. We are close to a high and barren ridge.

We cured Benigno, whose wound has a bit of pus in it, and I gave the Doctor an injection. As a result of the treatment, Benigno complained of pains in the night.

The radio reported that our two Cambas had been transferred to Camiri to act as witnesses in the Debray trial.
h = 2,000

OCTOBER 6

Scouting trips showed that there was a house very close, but also that there was water in a ravine further away. We made for that place and cooked all day beneath a large ledge which served as a roof, in spite of the fact that I was most uneasy because we had been in broad daylight near places that were quite densely populated and because we were stuck in a hollow. Since our meal took a long time, we decided to leave at dawn for a tributary near this little creek and to make a more thorough exploration from there to determine its future course.

The Cruz del Sur reported an interview with the Cambas; Orlando was a little less cunning. The Chilean radio gave a report of censored news, indicating that there are 1,800 men looking for us in the area.
h = 1,750

OCTOBER 7

We have completed the eleventh month since the guerrilla began. It was a day without complications, even bucolic, until 12:30, when an old woman herding her goats entered the canyon where we had camped and we had to take her prisoner. The woman has not given any trustworthy news about the soldiers, saying to every question that she doesn't know, and that she hasn't been past here for a long time. She only gave us information about the trails; as a result of her information, we estimate that we are about one league from Higueras and another from Jagüey and about two from Pucará. At 17:30, Inti, Aniceto and Pablito went to the old woman's house, where she had one crippled and one dwarf daughter. She was given 50 pesos and charged with not speaking a word; we don't have much hope that she will keep her promises. The seventeen of us went off under a small moon and the march was very tiresome and we left a lot of tracks in the canyon where we were; it has no houses nearby, but

156

there are some potato fields irrigated by ditches from the same stream. At 2:00 we halted to rest, because it was useless to go on advancing. El Chino becomes a real burden when we have to travel by night.

The army issued a strange report about the presence of 250 men in Serrano to stop the passage of the encircled men, who are said to number 37; they locate our hiding-place between the Acero and Oro rivers.

The news seems to be a red herring.
h=2,000

The end of the diary.
On October 8th, 1967, Che Guevara was wounded and captured.
He was later shot.

POSTSCRIPT

Guerrilla warfare in Bolivia is not dead!

It has just begun.

The Bolivian guerrillas are now fully on their way, and we will unflaggingly carry the struggle through to the brilliant victory of the revolutionary forces that will bring socialism to Latin America.

Our country has lived through — in principle — a revolutionary experience of undreamt continental proportions. The beginning of our struggle was accompanied by tragic adversity. The irreparable physical death of our friend and comrade, our Major Ernesto Che Guevara, as well as of many other fighters, has been a rude blow to us. They, who were the purest and noblest of our continent's generation, did not hesitate to offer up the only thing they could — their lives — on the altar of human redemption.

But these painful events, far from frightening us, strengthen our revolutionary awareness; increase our determination to fight for a just cause; make it stauncher; and forge, in the purifying and bloody crucible of war, new fighters and leaders, who will honour and pay homage to those who have already fallen.

We know what we are fighting for. We are not waging war for the sake of war. We are not wishful thinkers. We are not fighting for the sake of personal or party ambition. We have confidence in man as a human being.

Our single and final goal is the liberation of Latin America, which is more than our continent; it is rather our homeland, temporarily torn into twenty republics.

We are convinced that the dream of Bolívar and Che — that of uniting Latin America both politically and geographically — will be attained through armed struggle, which is the only dignified, honest, glorious, and irreversible method which will motivate the people. No other form of struggle is purer. Guerrilla warfare is the most effective and correct method of armed struggle.

For this reason, as long as there is a single honest man in Latin America, guerrilla warfare will not die. Armed struggle will surge ahead vigorously, until all of the people awake and rise up in arms against the common enemy, U.S. imperialism.

Guerrilla warfare in Bolivia is not dead; it has just begun. . . .

We have lost a battle, a battle in which the maximum leader of the oppressed people, Major Ernesto Che Guevara, gave his life.

But our war continues, and we will never stop, because we who fought at Che's side do not recognise the word ' surrender.' His blood and that of other fighters, spilled on the soil of Bolivia, will give life to the seed of liberation and will turn our continent into a volcano, spewing forth fire and destruction on imperialism.

We will be the triumphant Vietnam that Che, the romantic and heroic visionary, dreamed of and loved.

We are determined to win or die for these ideals.

Cuban comrades died for these ideals.

Peruvian comrades died for these ideals.

Argentine comrades died for these ideals.

Bolivian comrades died for these ideals.

Honour and glory for Tania, Joaquín, Juan Pablo Chang, Moisés Guevara, Jorge Vázquez, Aniceto Reynaga, Antonio Jiménez, and Coco Peredo; honour and glory for each and every one of those who died with weapons in hand, because they understood that, as Che said:

' Wherever death may surprise us, let it be welcome, so long as our battle cry reach some receptive ear and another hand reach out to pick up our weapons, and other men come forward to intone our funeral dirge with the staccato of machine-guns and new cries of battle and victory.'

Our banners bear crepe, but they will never be lowered.

The National Liberation Army considers itself the heir to the teachings and example of Che, the new Bolívar of Latin America.

Those who cravenly murdered him will never kill his thought and his example.

Let the imperialists and their lackeys withhold their songs of victory, because the war has not ended; it has just begun.

We will return to the mountains!

Bolivia will again resound to our cry of
VICTORY OR DEATH!
Bolivia, July, 1968   INTI PEREDO

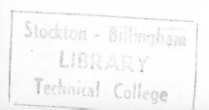

160